# Adopt A Lamb

# Adopt A Lamb

*David R. High*

**Books for Children of the World**
Oklahoma City, OK

Unless otherwise indicated, all scriptural quotations are from the *King James Version* of the Bible.

*Adopt-A-Lamb*
Published by:
Books for Children of the World
6701 N. Bryant
Oklahoma City, OK 73121
www.adoptalamb.org
ISBN 0-9661186-7-7

Second Printing: July 2003
Copyright © 2000 by David R. High
All rights reserved.
Reproduction of text in whole or in part without the express written consent by the author is not permitted and is unlawful according to the 1976 United States Copyright Act.

Cover design and book production by:
DB & Associates Design Group, Inc.
dba Double Blessing Productions
P.O. Box 52756, Tulsa, OK 74152
Cover illustration is protected by the 1976 United States Copyright Act.
Copyright © 2000 by DB & Associates Design Group, Inc.
Edited by Jenny Avery

Printed in the United States of America.

# Contents

*Introduction*

1. In the Beginning ...................................................... 1
2. What Must I Do To Be Saved ................................. 7
3. Worship and Praise ................................................ 13
4. Prayer ....................................................................... 19
5. Tithing and Giving ................................................. 27
6. Water Baptism ........................................................ 33
7. Faith Toward God .................................................. 39
8. Kings and Priests ................................................... 47
9. Eternal Judgment .................................................. 53
10. Scripture Reading ................................................ 61
11. Resurrection of the Dead ................................... 67
12 Fellowship ............................................................. 73
13. The Holy Spirit .................................................... 79
14. Laying on of Hands ............................................ 85

15. Forgiveness ..................................................91
16. Fasting .........................................................99
17. Repentance ................................................105
18. New Jerusalem ..........................................111
19. Witnessing ................................................117
20. Communion ..............................................123

# Introduction

Through the technologies of the 21st century, the good news of God's redemption for mankind from sin is being presented to ever increasing numbers of people. It seems, however, that a great need exists for a practical, systematic plan to teach the basic, foundational truths of the Christian faith to those who are trusting Jesus Christ for forgiveness of their sins. Some 20 years ago while pastoring a church, the inspiration for the *Adopt-A-Lamb* series came to me as I sought to simplify the process by which new converts matured. Since the commandment to make disciples is given to all believers, I tried to find a way to involve the whole church in the growth of these new additions to the Church.

It was decided that if we could involve the older members of our church in the growth process of the younger believers that there would be many benefits. Since the process would take about 20 weeks, the new lambs would not only have a grasp of the basics when they finished, they would go through the process with a mentor who would probably become their friend. We were convinced that this older brother or sister relationship would be a stabilizing force in the younger lambs' lives.

After identifying 20 basic principles of Christianity, we began to train the older members of the Church so they could, in turn, teach others. As the process began to unfold, we soon discovered an unexpected benefit. We found that, as the mentors began preparing to teach others, they were stirred to new levels of personal spiritual commitment. So often, the foundation principles that brought us life in the beginning of our own faith are neglected. The preparation that required the mentors to revisit these truths also brought back the life of a renewed faith.

Our hope is that, after you finish studying and embracing the basics of the Christian faith that are assembled in this book, you will find a young Christian and invest the time to pass on the torch of faith to him or her. We are convinced that once you find the joy of giving your faith to others, you will do it for the rest of your life. *Adopt-A-Lamb* is also available on our Web Site at:

*www.adoptalamb.org*

Through the web site you are able to interact with new believers anyplace in the world who have access to the internet. With a little imagination and the leadership of the Holy Spirit, you can participate in this great end-time harvest. Don't miss heaven's opportunity to be a part of what God is doing in the earth in your generation.

# Adopt A Lamb

## Lesson #1

# In the Beginning

Have you ever asked yourself how all of this started in the first place? How did man's journey begin? Where did God come from? Where are we going as the human race? As you work your way through these studies, many questions will be presented. As you and your sponsor discuss these issues that are vital to your success as a Christian, our desire is that you find the answers and begin to put them into practice in your life. After all, it is the living of your life by God's plan that will bring fulfillment to your existence here on earth and lead you to an eternity with God.

Remember that as we travel this journey together, our authority for all the life principles we will teach you will come from the Scriptures. Our hope is that by the time you finish this course, you will come to the same conclusion as we have. God's Word is true and it can be relied upon as the guide for your life. So anytime we refer you to a Scripture reference, please take the time to read it for yourself. By doing so, you will not only see for yourself that what we are teaching you is true, but you will also find that by the time we are finished, you will become familiar with the Bible as a reference book. So how did all this begin?

## Principle #1 — God is the Creator. That makes Him the owner.

The Bible says in Genesis Chapter one that in the beginning God said let there be light and there was light. When things were just beginning for man, God was already there. God is an eternal being. As difficult as it may be for our minds to comprehend, God has always been. In fact, the Bible says that God is the Creator of everything. In the first chapter of Genesis we are told how God made the heavens and earth and everything in them. That includes us.

When someone creates something, the act of creating makes the creator the owner. The Scriptures tell us that God owns the cattle on a thousand hills. Why? If God created them, He owns them. You will discover through this line of thinking that mankind has a tremendous responsibility to God. In *Genesis 1:27* the Bible tells us that God created us. The mere fact that we owe our very existence to someone is a humbling thought. Unless God had decided to bring us into existence, we wouldn't even be here. Think about that: God loved us enough, even before we acknowledged Him, to give us life so that we would have the opportunity to decide whether or not we would believe in Him.

## Principle #2 — Mankind needs a Savior.

Why did God create us? Mankind is such a mess. Why would God want to cause Himself so much grief by creating man? The answer to that question is simple, yet profound. God loves us. In fact, the Bible tells us that before we were born, God knew us. Think of that: Before you were even born, God knew your entire life with all its good and bad, and He still loved you enough to give you life.

In the beginning when God created man and placed him in the garden, the plan was for man to share his life with God forever. The garden was a perfect place. God wanted man to live there forever, enjoying what He had made for him. The rules in the garden were simple. Man was given freedom to use everything there with one exception. Man was not to eat from the tree of the knowledge of good and evil. As long as man obeyed, his life was blessed and wonderful. How much better could it get? Man was living in a perfect environment with a perfect partner and fellowshipping with a perfect God. Had there been no problems, Adam and Eve would still be alive today, and you could invite them over for dinner. Obviously, however, that isn't the case. Something happened that interrupted this idyllic setting.

In this perfect setting, something happened to turn the whole thing upside down. There was a part of God's creation that didn't follow the plan. Prior to Adam and Eve, God had made an anointed cherub who carried a lot of responsibility in heaven. His name was Lucifer. Because of his position, he came to believe he was as important as God Himself. He challenged God's authority and as a result was banished from heaven. God's judgment of him placed him under Adam's authority in the garden. Satan, as he became known, was so upset that he began encouraging Adam and Eve to question God's rules about living in the garden.

The question he asked of Adam and Eve is the same one He asks mankind today. "Hath God said?" When we are trying to decide how to live our lives, the struggle inside us is the same: Are we really accountable to God or not? As Adam and Eve started questioning God's rules, eventually they arrived at a dangerous conclusion. By deciding they could make their own decisions about how to conduct their lives, they fell prey to the same way of thinking that caused a breach in the relationship between God and Satan. Once man decided to make his own decisions, submitting to God's rules became difficult. Eventually man decided to do what he wanted and ignored God's rules.

That scenario pretty much describes the condition we find man in today. Mankind decided that he was better equipped to make his own decisions, and he turned his back on God's leadership. Once he had made that decision, man found himself separated from God just like Satan was. The decision to reject God's leadership and make his own decisions about how to run his own life was called *sin*. The problem with sin was that once it had been committed, there was no way to remedy the problem. Man could not simply say, "Whoops!" and fix the problem himself. A violation had occurred for which a price had to be paid. The problem for man was that, since it was God's law that had been broken, it was up to God to decide what price would be required to pay for the offense. God's price was the offering of sinless blood. However, once mankind had sinned, there was no longer anyone in the human race who was qualified to pay the price.

## Principle #3 — Man cannot save himself.

The results of man's actions were disastrous. He tended to think that he was the only one who would be affected by the decisions he had made. In this case nothing could have been further from the truth. When man decided to lead himself, everything around him began to suffer the consequences of his decision.

### *Relationship with God*

The first casualty of man's decision was the loss of an open relationship with God. The Bible says that whoever finds God, finds life (Proverbs 8:35). When man lost his relationship with God, he lost eternal life. In fact, God placed cherubim with flaming swords east of Eden to guard the way to the tree of life. Sin cost man his source of life.

## Family

Sin has a cascading effect that multiplies if it is not dealt with. In our continuing story, we see that once the primary relationship with God had been broken, the problem of sin spread to Adam's family. One of his first two children killed the other one. People have been murdering each other ever since. Because man was then presently making his own rules, he could change them whenever it was convenient. Today, we understand that this ability to change the rules has left us with shifting standards which breed insecurity. Consequently, divorce is accepted when it is convenient. Abandoning children is justified. Abuse is explained away. Mankind desperately needs divine intervention to put the pieces of broken relationships back together.

## Nature

Man's rebellion disrupted God's balance and brought chaos to all of creation. The former rulership of life had been replaced by death. Everything from man's health to his environment began to suffer a downward spiral to destruction. Even the social structures that were intended to bring quality and fulfillment to life were left empty. Today's consequences? Polluted water, dirty air, aborted children; Godless courts, schools, and governments — all testify of the results of man's failed attempt to determine his own destiny. Without a continuing relationship with God, man is doomed to the futility of trying an endless list of good ideas that end in even bigger problems. Communism, an entitlement approach to welfare reform, and schools without morals have all led to disaster. Partnership with Heaven is the only way to find lasting solutions to man's need for leadership.

When man realizes that there is a problem with his life, he begins to look for a solution within himself. People tend to turn to good deeds to help them feel better. People go through seasons of personal resolve promising themselves that they are going to reform. The sad truth is, however, that no amount of good works can bridge the gap sin created between God and man.

The wonderful part of this story is that God had a plan to solve the problem before we needed it. When the separation occurred between God and man, we were not the only ones who were hurt. God was hurt! Difficult as it may be to understand, He *wants* to fellowship with us, and He loved us enough that He arranged to pay the price for our sins Himself. He was so confident His plan would work that He went to prepare a place for us to live with Him forever.

*Discussion Points:*

1. What was God's plan for mankind from the beginning?

2. How did man disobey God?

3. What was Satan's role in this disobedience?

4. Who is going to solve the problem?

*Memory Verse:*

**All things were made by Him; and without Him was not anything made that was made.**

**John 1:3**

## Lesson #2
# What Must I Do To Be Saved?

Since the beginning of time, man has struggled with the question of what will happen to him when he dies. Searching for the answer to that question has produced a variety of possibilities born out of wishful thinking and imagination. Some think there is nothing after this life, while others think that in the afterlife, everyone will be swept away to a beautiful place where happiness exists forever. While I can appreciate the fact that there may be good reasons why people come up with personal beliefs which make them comfortable, there is only one true future reality. What one believes only has significance if it is based on the truth.

Remember, man's search of God's truths must be based on the reality revealed in the Scriptures and not upon fantasies born out of his imagination. When a person stands before God, it won't matter how creative his beliefs were; it will only matter whether or not he believed in God's plan. In the end, it is only by believing in and acting on that plan that he will gain entrance into eternity with God.

### Principle #1 — God has a plan.

Throughout history the principle of justice has been valued by all civilizations. Mankind learned at an early age that disobedience has consequences and requires punishment. When things go wrong, somebody has to pay. This feeling is so ingrained in society that when a person disobeys, his conscience causes him to feel guilt over his actions. Man has so desperately tried to find a way of living apart from God's oversight, he has sacrificed his own peace of mind in his struggle to live a self-determined life. Man finds himself striving to get what he wants, only to discover, once he gets it, that he didn't want what he got. A person who lives life by making up his own rules is a person who will live life unfulfilled.

The Bible teaches us that God created us with a purpose in mind. In the Garden of Eden that purpose suffered a tremendous setback. Satan's deception and lies led man to question and reject God's rulership. In thinking that he could lead a self-determined life, man's rebellion against God simply caused him to exchange one ruler for another. When man submitted himself to Satan, he removed himself from God's loving protection. The horror of that decision caused a separation that continues to this day.

Man then found himself on one side of a great divide and God on the other. How could man ever rectify the wrong? What could he do to pay for the offense?

When mankind in general finally realized that they were the problem, some turned their guilt into good works in an effort to pay for their actions. Some responded differently by giving up all hope of ever finding forgiveness and began living a wild, self-destructive lifestyle. Some, on the other hand, went into denial and began to blame others. Eventually, however, all reached the same conclusion: There is nothing a person can do from his side of the problem to fix the problem. Good works, guilt, blame, hopelessness or even a self-invented version of life after death all come up short.

Since there was nothing that could be done from man's side to resolve the sin problem, the only hope he had was that something could be done from God's side to adequately address the division between God and man. There is a perfect example in the Scriptures of this very situation.

In *Genesis 14:8* Abraham was asked by God to sacrifice his son Isaac. This was Abraham's son through whom the covenant was to extend to the next generation. As Abraham made preparation to sacrifice his son, an amazing thing happened. Just as he was about to plunge the knife into Isaac, a ram appeared, caught in a thicket nearby. It was this ram that became the sacrifice instead of Isaac. You see, Isaac's death would have accomplished nothing. Even though Abraham was willing, the price he was prepared to pay wouldn't have begun to settle the debt he owed. It was God who supplied the sacrifice.

When God viewed all the contortions men went through in their feeble attempts to make peace with Him, He saw that they all fell horribly short of meeting the requirements. Because God loves us with His eternal love and compassion and remembers our frame that we are dust (*Psalm 103*), He made provision by sending a sacrifice that would meet the requirements for us.

In the fullness of time, God sent His own Son to be that sacrifice for us. Jesus Christ was God's own Son who came into this world, born of a virgin and who lived a sinless life. He was sent to destroy the curse of sin by allowing Himself to pay the ultimate price. Jesus took upon Himself the sins of the world and died on a Roman cross. The Bible says that the just payment for sin is death. By paying the price for our sins, He satisfied the requirements of restoring our relationship with God.

Once the price was paid, death could not hold Him because He was sinless. The power of death is sin. Since Jesus died without sin, death could not keep Him, and He arose from the dead.

What the Bible tells us next is quite remarkable. This Good News is expressed in the answer Paul gave the Philippian jailer when he asked, "What must I do to be saved?" Paul said, "Believe on the Lord Jesus Christ and you shall be saved." What does it mean to believe in Jesus? The answer is simple, yet profound. Since God provided the complete solution to our sin problem, what else can we add to His provision? Nothing. Then what is required on our part? We must believe that what God did through Jesus' life, death and resurrection was enough to satisfy our spiritual debt.

Let me give you a practical example. Suppose you had a relative who died, and you were told he had left you a large sum of money. The attorney told you that an account had been opened at the local bank in your name and that all you had to do was present proper identification, and the money was yours. What would be your response? You would either believe it or you wouldn't. If you believed what you were told, you would go to the bank and take out what was yours. If you didn't believe what you were told, the money would simply sit in the bank until you died. You could be wealthy and yet live your whole life as a pauper if you never believed the truth about what you were told.

When Jesus died for us, He really did pay the price for our sins. The sad news is that most people don't believe it's true. Jesus paid the bill; yet most people continue to live as if the deposit was never made into their account. It is heartbreaking to see people trying to pay a debt with their lives, when that debt has already been paid.

To actually accept God's gift of eternal life requires a leap of faith that is humbling. We may believe Jesus was a real person who lived over two thousand years ago. Simply believing He existed, however, isn't life saving. I believe George Washington existed, but that belief doesn't do anything for me *personally*. What we must believe is that Jesus actually *was* who He said He was; then we must begin to *act on* what we believe. This *acting on what we believe* is a simple definition of *faith*.

What are you going to put your faith in for your eternity? Our hope is that you believe the truth about Jesus and take the appropriate action to accept God's gift of eternal life.

*Salvation Plan:*

1. Acknowledge to God that you are a sinner. (Romans 3:10, 23)

2. Repent. (Decide to stop living your own way and submit your life to God.) (Acts 2:38)

3. Ask God's forgiveness for living outside His laws. (Proverbs 21:2)

4. Accept God's gift of eternal life. (John 10:28)

5. Decide to live the rest of your life in a way that pleases God. (John 14:15)

6. Use the Scriptures to determine how God wants you to live. (2 Timothy 3:16,17)

7. Tell others about your decision. (Matthew 28:19)

*What are the benefits of salvation?* (Isaiah 53:3-5)

1. Forgiveness — guilt free living (1 John 1:9)
2. Help in living this life here and now (2 Peter 1:4)
3. Eternal life (Romans 6:23)

*Discussion Points:*

1. Why does man need a Savior?
2. What does it mean to trust God for your salvation?

3. What are we saved from?
4. What are we saved to?

*Memory Verse:*

For God so loved the world that He gave His only begotten Son, that whosoever believeth in Him should not perish but have everlasting life.

For God sent not His Son into the world to condemn the world; but that the world through Him might be saved.

**John 3:16,17**

## Lesson #3
# Worship and Praise

Throughout history, mankind has exhibited a trait common to all ages and cultures. He seems to have an inborn need to find something bigger than himself to believe in. This is a most unusual shared feature, in light of the fact that unsaved man desperately wants to reassure himself that there is nothing worthy of his worship. While man is trying to justify to himself that he is accountable to no one but himself, his very nature betrays this misplaced belief and testifies of his need to worship God.

Worship is defined as respect paid to a higher power, extreme devotion, or intense love. While worship is normally associated with God, if man chooses not to acknowledge God's rightful place in his life, then other things become the objects of worship. Man was created with a need and capacity to worship. Remove God as the object of that worship and other things emerge. Ask yourself; look around; do you see mankind giving extreme devotion to anything besides God?

You don't have to look very far to see man giving extreme devotion to everything except God. Modern society worships youth, beauty, education, entertainment, self-determination, prosperity, Godless ideologies, and many other things in his futile attempt to set God aside. In the final analysis, however, none of these pretenders to the throne have the capability to love man back. Nothing truly satisfies or fulfills until man surrenders his heart and learns to give his extreme devotion to God.

## Principle #1 — Man was created with a need to worship, and he will worship something.

In the Scriptures there are numerous examples of man's attempts to create a system of worship rather than simply follow God's plan. Cain, who was the son of Adam and Eve, offered a sacrifice to God, but not according to God's plan. In *Genesis 4:1-12* Cain offered a sacrifice from his crop, even though God required a sacrifice from the flock. Like so many people today, Cain wanted to worship, but on his own terms. People want to decide the limits to their devotion, so they make up their own rules. Cain offered an unacceptable sacrifice that was rejected by God. This rejection upset Cain so much that he killed his own brother in a fit of jealously.

## Principle #2 — Worship in a way acceptable to God.

Once, when the people of Israel were on their journey from Egypt to the Promised Land, they fell victim to another human shortcoming in worship. As they waited at the bottom of the mountain for Moses to return, they became impatient. While Moses spoke with God on the mountain — Moses was up there for forty days — the rumor began circulating among the people that he was dead and wouldn't return. In like manner, we can see this story's parallel to our own lives. In the absence of a quick response to our prayers, we might incorrectly conclude that God isn't going to answer. When Israel came to the conclusion that God wasn't going to speak to them, they assumed control of their own destiny.

They decided to build themselves an idol. The result was a golden calf to which they decided to give their affections.

Any thinking person surely can see that giving worship to something he has made with his own hands is hopeless. As silly as it may seem, people do it every day. People create businesses, then give them extreme devotion. Every decision they make is based on what is best for their businesses. This kind of living places God and their families in a secondary position to their first love. Men create ideologies and give themselves so completely to them that nothing else in life matters. Communism or democracy can be honored above God's way of doing things. Men can invest so much time and effort in their yards or their golf swings that they don't even realize they have shifted their affections to things that can never bring fulfillment.

## Principle #3 — If you made it, don't worship it.

*Matthew 15:1-15* gives God's opinion on the matter. The Israelites had deteriorated to the point that their worship of God was empty and predictable. They had made so many rules and interpretations of rules that their part became more important than God's part. God's opinion was that their worship was in vain. Their traditions and interpretations of God's Word now overshadowed the Word itself. The application? Before you decide to add something to your belief system and include it in your worship, make sure it is supported and validated by the Scriptures.

Remember that Satan's downfall was that he wanted to be the object of worship rather than a worshipper. If you create your own system of worship, you may well be playing into Satan's hands by denying God the worship He deserves. Satan's nature has never changed. In the tribulation when the antichrist is revealed, he will work all kinds of wonders in an effort to draw people into worshipping him. If Satan's desire is to divert worship to himself, how can we avoid the pitfalls and give God the worship He deserves and do it in the way He desires?

The Christian life is an affair of the heart and not one of simple outward obedience. God is more concerned with motive and attitude than He is with adherence to a set of rules. *John 4:24* says that God is seeking true worshippers who will worship Him in spirit and in truth. This true worship is achieved when the believer surrenders his inner self to God's will. You see, God wants a people who will give their hearts and affections to Him because they love Him. Some people mistakenly think of God as some kind of invisible butler. It is easy to have affection for someone who can do things for you. The higher relationship, however, is born out of honoring and respecting someone's character. Once you come to know God by observing His character, your love for Him will allow you to give the deepest part of yourself in true worship.

This is perhaps one of the most difficult truths in all of Christianity, yet once it becomes part of you, it is totally liberating. When you know God well enough to say, "I trust You," your life takes on a whole new dimension. Trust requires no evidence other than to know you are doing what God wants you to do. When your finances are a mess, you will be able to say, "God, I don't know where this is taking me, but I know You will be there." When you see others being blessed and, in your need, you are still able to be joyful in what you have, that gratitude is an act of true worship.

To say to God, "No matter what comes my way, I know You have my best interest in mind," requires a relationship. There may be times in your life when things don't make sense. You ask every question, repent of every possible offense, forgive everyone who has wronged you, and still the answers won't come. You hurt and don't know why. In times like these, if you can retreat into the love of God because you trust Him, you will find emotional support the world doesn't have.

King David found just such a hiding place when he returned to Ziklag to find his house burned, his wealth stolen, and his wives and children kidnapped. Just when the reader thinks things couldn't possibly get any worse for David, his own men blame him and want to kill him. However, in the middle of the lowest of lows, David was, because of his relationship with God, able to retreat into his abiding trust in God. One of the most remarkable verses in Scripture tells of David's response to his circumstances. *First Samuel 30:6* says, "...and David encouraged himself in the Lord his God." With absolutely no external evidence or support, David was able to resort to his trust in God to give him encouragement and direction. The end of the story is that, not only was David's life spared, but also, he and his men defeated their enemies and recovered all their families and wealth.

## Principle #4 — True worship is life-giving.

If you have a friend who treats you like God treated David, wouldn't you think it appropriate to express your appreciation occasionally? It is not only reasonable, but life-giving when you find expression for the feelings you have for God. There are many ways to tell God you love and trust Him. The important thing is that you do it.

There are many outward ways that people show what is going on inside their hearts. When people worship, they might sing, dance, cry, laugh, kneel, jump, raise their hands, give offerings, pray or do any number of things. These outward expressions of the heart's worship is what praise is made of. While outward expressions of praise (or what looks like praise) may not necessarily mean worship is in the heart, when true worship is in the heart of the believer, praise will find a way out.

*Discussion Points:*
1. What is worship?
2. Why was Cain's offering rejected?
3. Where did David find his strength?
4. What is the difference between praise and worship?

*Memory Verse:*
**Give unto the Lord the glory due His name; worship the Lord in the beauty of holiness.**
**Psalm 29:2**

## Lesson #4
# Prayer

One of the cornerstones of the Christian life is the ability of the believer to communicate directly with God. It is quite a remarkable concept when you think about it. A rather small, insignificant part of God's creation (man) is given access to the very throne room of the universe and invited in to have a talk with the Creator of the universe about anything important to him. There are some misconceptions, however, about how prayer works. As we search the Scriptures, we hope to expand your understanding of the unprecedented opportunity offered to the believer by the power of prayer.

Prayer in its simplest form is just talking with God. In its full expression it is much more. As in the development of any relationship, language expresses a full range of emotions. When two people communicate, they may express joy, fear or hope or try to work out a problem or just share information. The same is true of our prayer life. When we talk with God, it can be for a wide variety of reasons.

Usually prayer is centered on sharing some need or seeking direction about some area of our life. Life is full of enough surprises to present plenty of opportunities to appeal to Heaven for help. Financial downturns, sickness, hurting relationships and demonic attacks are all opportunities for us to call on our heavenly Father to rally to our aid. When we are in the middle of one of these problems, we might not always be in the frame of mind to offer up a nice quiet, sweet prayer. Sometimes, an extreme circumstance calls for an extreme response. But before we explore the variety of ways we pray, let's take a few moments to see just how prayer works.

Have you ever wondered what it is about prayer that changes things? You speak words to an invisible listener and expect that somehow a response will come. Just how do your words enact a response? To help you understand, let me use an example from the other side of the spiritual world.

If a witch doctor issues a curse against someone and the curse causes harm, how does that work? What is it about words that allow them to change things? The Bible says that life and death are in the power of the tongue. It seems a reasonable conclusion that the demons that are in partnership with the witch doctor are empowered by the words of the witch doctor as messengers of destruction. If the one cursed by the witch doctor has no defense, then the demons exact their evil on the victim. As unpleasant as this may seem, it happens all the time. People are thoughtlessly speaking evil of others more often than you may think. When rumors are spread or evil is wished on someone, evil is empowered to carry out its hurt on the unsuspecting subject of the hatred.

What would happen in this same scenario if evil were empowered against a Christian? Some person issues words against one of God's people. The demons arrive at the house of a righteous man empowered by the words of someone who wishes evil on them. Can they deliver the curse?

There is a tremendous promise in *Isaiah 54:17*. It says:

**"No weapon formed against you shall prosper, and every tongue that rises against you in judgment you**

shall condemn. This is the heritage of the servant of the Lord."

It is self-evident that, the curse of evil, when met by righteousness, finds an impossible task. Remember, God is the Creator, and it is part of His creation that fell to rebellion and brought evil into this world. The fact that God is greater than any other power is comforting when you find yourself attacked. If God were not greater, why would you want to serve Him? After all, He is the one who promised to make all things work together for your good. So, evil knocks at your door and is answered by the righteousness of God. Can evil leave its package of mischief? Absolutely not. Not if you refuse to receive it.

**"Submit yourselves therefore to God. Resist the devil, and he will flee from you."**

**James 4:7**

It is your heritage as a believer to send evil packing. Remember, Isaiah tells *you* to condemn every word of judgment against you. Don't ever doubt Heaven's resolve to back you in resisting evil. As one of God's children, you can and should expect your partnership with Heaven to make a difference.

What happens to all that mischief if evil powers are not able to leave their misery? If the package is undeliverable, it is returned to the sender. Those words don't just vanish because the righteous stood against them and refused to receive them. They still have action in them.

**"Death and life are in the power of the tongue: and they that love it shall eat the fruit thereof."**

**Proverbs 18:21**

That is why the most miserable people in the world are those who are always wishing evil on others. They are sending out package after package of ill will only to have some of them returned because they are unable to be delivered to the righteous. While they are speaking words of mistrust against others, they can't understand why others are suspicious of and mistrust them. When demons return the hurt, mistrust, sickness, suspicion, anger, guilt, etc. to the unrighteous sender, they are defenseless against the calamities they have unleashed on themselves.

"Arise, O LORD, in thine anger, lift up thyself because of the rage of mine enemies: and awake for me to the judgment that thou hast commanded.

The LORD shall judge the people: judge me, O LORD, according to my righteousness, and according to mine integrity that is in me.

Oh let the wickedness of the wicked come to an end; but establish the just: for the righteous God trieth the hearts and reins.

My defense is of God, which saveth the upright in heart.

God judgeth the righteous, and God is angry with the wicked every day."

Psalm 7:6,8-11

"Behold, he (the wicked) travaileth with iniquity, and hath conceived mischief, and brought forth falsehood.

He made a pit, and digged it, and is fallen into the ditch which he made.

His mischief shall return upon his own head, and his violent dealing shall come down upon his own pate (head)."

Psalm 7:14-16

You know that evil always tries to imitate righteousness. So if evil words can move the powers of darkness to harm, what ability of the righteous are they imitating? Prayer is the wondrous expression of our partnership with Heaven. In prayer the believer is invited to lift his voice to God in many different expressions. We are told that we should always bless and curse not (Romans 12:4). When we come before God in prayer and begin to ask God to bless others, what happens to our words? The invisible, righteous, spiritual world takes notice, and when prayer is made according to the will of God, angels are empowered to dispense the blessing for which we are calling.

If you are calling to Heaven to see good things happen to others, that is called a prayer of blessing. When you genuinely want to see benefits delivered to someone who needs help, angels are empowered to deliver blessings and are sent out to make their delivery. We are told to always bless and not to curse. Unlike the wicked, when our packages are delivered to the righteous, we are happy. The blessing we sought for someone has been delivered, and we rejoice because they are blessed. But what if the person we are praying for is not in a position to receive the blessing? Herein lies one of the unexpected benefits of doing things God's way.

You find yourself praying for someone who is not in fellowship with God and the package of blessings for some reason cannot be delivered. What happens to the package? It too is returned to sender just like the undeliverable packages of the wicked. The blessings you were genuinely praying would be delivered to the one in need are now brought back to you. The happiest people I know are those who are always seeking to bless others. Do you see why God wants you to always bless and not to curse? By blessing others you can never lose. If they are blessed, you are happy. If they can't receive the blessing, for whatever reason, it is returned to you.

Understand that the words that come out of your mouth have tremendous power. In the same way that spiritual beings are empowered to bless or curse others, your words have power through prayer in other ways. Because God has invited us to communicate with Him as often as we want, it would be foolish not to accept His offer. We have been invited to appeal to Heaven for advice or help when we find ourselves in need. Think about it. Who wouldn't want God's advice?

We might want to talk to God for a number of reasons. A few of these might include the following:

- To ask for forgiveness — When you feel guilt from inappropriate behavior you can express your desire to correct that behavior and ask forgiveness from God for the offense.

- To intercede for others — You can appeal to God to stand between a person and his problem, whether it be one of finances, health, relationships, demonic attack, weak character, etc..

- To give thanks — When you find yourself overcome with gratitude for all God has done for you, it seems only appropriate to express your feelings of appreciation to Him.

- To pray in the Spirit — Remember God is Spirit (John 4:24). There are times when it is entirely appropriate for your spirit to communicate directly with God on a spiritual level. When this happens, there are times when you may find yourself speaking in a language you don't understand (1 Corinthians 13:1). This praying in the spirit, or in a heavenly language, is a season of intimate fellowship between your spirit and God's. When this occurs, you will find that it is as if you were able to push a spiritual reset button. This spirit to Spirit communion gives your inner man reassurance that God truly is your partner in this life.

There is an example of a model prayer in the Scriptures. Jesus told His disciples that, when they prayed, the prayer should be something like the example given in *Matthew 6:9-13*. This sample prayer, often referred to as the Lord's Prayer, includes honoring God, requesting provision, asking for forgiveness, seeking guidance, desiring protection and acknowledging God's ownership.

However you express yourself to God, find time to speak with Him often. It is through His wisdom that life makes sense.

*Discussion Points:*
1. What is prayer?
2. Why should I always bless and not curse others?
3. Why should I give thanks?
4. What is the value of fellowship with God's Spirit?

*Memory Verse:*

**After this manner therefore pray ye: Our Father which art in heaven, Hallowed be thy name.**

**Thy kingdom come. Thy will be done in earth, as it is in heaven.**

**Give us this day our daily bread.**

**And forgive us our debts, as we forgive our debtors.**

**And lead us not into temptation, but deliver us from evil: For thine is the kingdom, and the power, and the glory, for ever. Amen.**
**Matthew 6:9-13**

## Lesson #5
# Tithing and Giving

One of the most controversial topics in Christian circles is how to handle your money. While the Bible has a lot to say on the subject, people tend to have strong opinions that have more control over their financial lives than the Scriptures do. I can assure you that God has a plan for your finances, and His plan will work. The challenge for all of us is do we trust God enough to do things His way? Many of the truths we will discuss in this series may, at first glance, seem to be impossible and impractical. Your mind will tend to reject new ways of doing things. Don't be too quick to write this one off. It could change your life as much as forgiveness or any of the other principles you will discover in these studies.

### Principle #1 — Tithing acknowledges God's ownership and partnership.

Everything we have is a gift from God. When He created this world in the beginning, He supplied it with everything we would need to survive and prosper (Philippians 4:19). The air we breathe, the food we eat and the lives we enjoy were all a part of His plan from the beginning. As the Creator of everything we see and use to survive, God has established certain rules by which we are to live. You see, God doesn't mind if we use His creation to live, but He does expect for us to acknowledge His ownership. One of the ways He has chosen for us to honor Him is through tithing.

The word *tithe* literally means a tenth. God blesses us out of His abundance; then He expects us to give 10% of our income back to Him in appreciation of His partnership in our lives. The first reaction to such a proposal often is one of complete denial. Our feeble minds struggle with the possibility of living on 90% of which others live. We have difficulty understanding how such a plan could work when we are having trouble keeping our financial heads above water without tithing. The missing piece in our thought process is that tithing brings God into our finances as a partner. If I were to tell you that I would like to go into business with you and I would supply everything you needed to succeed, what percentage of your profits would you be willing to give in return? That is exactly what God has done for us. All He wants is 10% of our increase to continue the partnership.

## Principle #2 — Tithes and offerings provide for God's work on earth.

The first instance of tithing we find in the Bible is found in *Genesis 14:6* when Abraham paid tithes to Melchizedek, the priest. Abraham had just returned from a war where he and his men had defeated five northern kings. The first thing he did when he returned was to seek out the man of God and pay what he felt he owed his Partner. Abraham knew he owed his success to God, and he wanted to be sure he took care of that obligation first. The commandment to pay your tithe first should not be ignored. You see, God doesn't need your money, but He does desire your appreciation and gratitude for the part He plays in your life.

Since tithing is a commandment, you cannot give your tithe; you must pay it as you would any other obligation. This is a very important distinction to take note of for future reference. You can't give what you owe. Why is tithing included in God's plan? Does He need our money? The obvious answer is, "No." God doesn't need our money, but He does need our trust and obedience. Tithing is also one of the ways God provides for His work on the earth.

Where are you supposed to pay your tithes? The Bible says in *Malachi 3:10* that we are to bring our tithes into the storehouse. The storehouse concept in the Old Testament was a place where you could deposit excess in good times so that in bad times you could withdraw if you had a need. The Bible also teaches that we are to share with those who teach us in the Word. To put all that into a New Testament context, we should pay our tithes where we are being instructed in the Word and where in times of need we can find help. This indicates that there is a relationship with the place that receives your tithes. While there certainly are many good national ministries, few would qualify as a proper destination for your tithes. Anything given to such a ministry would more properly fall into the category of offerings.

The Bible says in *Luke 6:38,* "Give, and it shall be given unto you; good measure, pressed down, and shaken together, and running over shall men give into your bosom." This giving doesn't kick in until you have gone past the 10% tithe. Once you have paid the tithe that you owe, you can then begin investing in the Kingdom by giving offerings. The joy of paying your bill is one thing, but the joy of giving is something else altogether. God loves a cheerful giver. Don't hand over your tithe to an individual. You may find yourself trying to pay your bill to someone you don't owe. Pay your tithe first in the way God intended, and then if you want, invest an offering in an individual.

Have you ever wondered what happens to your money once you have given it to the church? The Scriptures tell us that the tithe and offerings received by the priests were used for four primary purposes.

First, the funds were used to care for the house of God. All the expenses and upkeep of the temple came from the tithes and offerings. As you read the Scriptures, you will find that the place of worship was quite elaborate. The elaborate furnishings of His house did not offend God, and He expected for it to be maintained properly.

Second, the funds were to be used to provide for the care of the priests. The priesthood of Levi cared for the temple, and they were forbidden to engage in normal commerce. They were permitted, however, to partake of the tithes and offerings of the people. This was their inheritance.

Third, the priests administered the funds for the care of the widows and orphans. There were then, as there are now, widows and orphans who needed help and financial assistance. The priests were to see that those who had genuine needs were treated fairly and with respect.

Fourth, the priests were also to care for the strangers at the gate. There are always those among us who may not believe exactly as we do and from time to time need help. God's plan includes reaching beyond our own to others on the outside who need to know the love of God.

In a New Testament context the funds received by a church should cover the expenses of the church building, the salaries of the church staff, the care of needy people in the congregation, and the costs of reaching out to the world through evangelism. If all the people of God were faithful in their tithes and offerings, there would be more than enough to complete the job before us.

## Principle #3 — Financial partnership with God blesses all aspects of your life.

What benefit comes to those who are obedient to the commandment to tithe and give offerings? In *Malachi 3:10* God issues the most amazing challenge. He says that if you will do what He asks with your tithes and offerings, He is willing to be put to the test. He challenges you to prove Him.

> "Bring ye all the tithes into the storehouse, that there may be meat in mine house, and prove me now herewith, saith the LORD of hosts, if I will not open you the windows of heaven, and pour you out a blessing, that there shall not be room enough to receive it."
>
> **Malachi 3:10**

No place else in the Scriptures can I find a place in which God offers to prove a promise. He says that if you do what He asks, He will open up the windows of Heaven and pour out a blessing, that you will not have room enough to receive it. God has issued the challenge. I encourage you to find out for yourself.

In the next verse He says that He will rebuke the devourer for our sakes. What is the devourer? You do know that to live by God's standards puts you at odds with the world's way of doing things. The world is under the control of a curse. That curse steals the blessing out of life. People work hard only to have the reward of their labor taken away by one misfortune after another. God promises that the cycle of misfortune can be broken, and you will actually be able to enjoy a different way of life.

Financial partnership with God brings the promise of seeing a return for your labor. When you plant a crop, you can expect to benefit from the harvest. Your crop will not drop its fruit before its time. You buy a used car and can fully expect that it will last long and serve you well. God, in fact, is able to cause all things to work together for your good. Your house doesn't burn down. Your health is good. Even when you come under attack, God is able to bring an unexpected favorable outcome. The favor of God becomes so obvious that all those around you will call you blessed. Does it sound too good to be true? God issued the challenge. Put Him to the test and see for yourself. Be sure you give the seed of obedience enough time to grow before you draw your final conclusions. Tithe, give and stand on the promises of God's Word. You will not be disappointed.

*Discussion Points:*

1. What does the word *tithe* mean?
2. What message do you give to God when you tithe?
3. What does the church do with the money?
4. How are you benefited from financial partnership with God?

*Memory Verse:*

**Give, and it shall be given unto you; good measure, pressed down, and shaken together, and running over, shall men give into your bosom.**

**Luke 6:38**

## Lesson #6
# Water Baptism

When Jesus was about to return to Heaven after His resurrection, He gave a very specific commandment to His disciples. It is recorded in Matthew 28:19,20 and reads as follows:

> "Go ye therefore, and teach all nations, baptizing them in the name of the Father, and of the Son, and of the Holy Ghost:
>
> Teaching them to observe all things whatsoever I have commanded you: and, lo, I am with you alway, even unto the end of the world. Amen."

When believers went out to tell others about their relationship with God, some of those who listened to the message would want to become followers of Christ also. Part of the process of making the commitment to follow Christ included being baptized. Unless you understand the significance of this event, it may seem unimportant. As with any other of the ceremonies or traditions of the Christian faith, if you don't understand why something is being done, it will be of little benefit to you. If you don't understand, always ask your sponsor or someone in your church why things are being done. Understanding the meaning of these events will allow you to participate with faith and confidence in the significance of the event rather than just simply going through the motions.

## What Is Baptism?

The phrase *to baptize* means "to plunge under" or "to dip." New believers are to be plunged under water as part of their commitment. This is not just some initiation ritual. Baptism has a great deal of meaning as it relates to the events that take place when someone commits his life to follow Christ. When you decide to become a Christian, you have decided to change your whole way of life. The essence of that decision is to adopt the teachings and life example of Jesus Christ as the model by which you will live. Living an independent, self-determined life ends. You are saying with your commitment, that from this point forward, you want to live your life in a manner that will be pleasing and acceptable to God.

In a real sense you are ceasing one way of life and starting to live by a new standard. The Bible calls this decision "dying to self." In exchange for forgiveness of your offenses and being given the gift of eternal life, God expects you to live your life in such a way that He would approve. To see if a decision or action would be acceptable to Him, read your Bible, talk to Him about it (pray), and if you are still having trouble, talk to your pastor.

I am sure you understand that most people in the world don't live this way. Most people don't care what God thinks about the way they live. To live your life to please God requires you to ask God's help. We are not talking about a New Year's resolution of trying hard to do better; we are talking about becoming a new person. It is not surprising that when people find this life-changing relationship with God, they are often misunderstood. After all, they are no longer the person they used to be.

Water baptism is a very appropriate way of demonstrating this life-changing decision. The person you used to be is becoming someone new. This dying to the old way you used to live and beginning to live by a new standard is proclaimed in baptism. The Bible says we are buried with Christ in baptism. What do you do with something that is dead? You bury it.

After Jesus took upon Himself the sins of the world and died on the cross, He was buried. The sins of the world put Him into the grave, but He arose victorious over sin. When we decide to follow Christ, the same thing happens to us.

In a baptismal service a pastor or another Christian goes into the water with you. He lays you into the water until you are covered. This is a symbolic way of saying that you are dead to your old way of life. Then the pastor raises you up out of the water to show that you are rising to a new life, leaving the old life behind. It is also a way of saying that your sins have been washed away. There is nothing magical about the water. There is, however, something empowering in the public statement about your intent to live a new kind of life. In being obedient to be publicly baptized, you are saying to any and all that you are committed to the decision you have made to the Christian life.

This public statement is so important that John baptized Jesus Himself in the Jordan River at the beginning of His ministry. When John the Baptist saw Jesus approaching him, he asked what His intentions were. Jesus said He had come to be baptized. Because John knew who Jesus was, he responded that he (John) needed to be baptized by Jesus. Jesus responded that He must fulfill all righteousness (set the right example) and was baptized by John.

From that point forward, when new believers made their decision to live this new way, baptism was a part of the process. There is no saving grace in the act of baptism. Believers are baptized not to be saved, but as a public testimony that they are saved.

There was an Ethiopian eunuch returning to his home by chariot in *Acts 8:36*. As he was traveling, he was also reading the Scriptures that described the life of Jesus. God arranged for Philip to meet with the man as he traveled. Their conversation led to an explanation of Jesus' life, death and resurrection. When the eunuch understood what the Scriptures said, he made the decision to commit his life to follow Jesus' teachings and life example. He became a Christian. The first thing he wanted to do after that decision was to be baptized. He turned to Philip and asked what was there to prevent him from being baptized? He even mentioned the fact that there was a lot of water nearby. Philip let him know that there was nothing to keep him from the public statement of his newfound faith. They stopped the chariot, and Philip baptized him right there.

On another occasion in *Acts 10*, Peter was called to Cornelius' house to tell them about Jesus. As Peter was in the middle of his message, those present responded to what they heard and believed what Peter was telling them. They believed and even began to worship in other languages. This miraculous occurrence was all the evidence Peter needed to determine that what he was witnessing was Heaven's acceptance of the faith of those present. In fact he reported later to the apostles in Jerusalem that he could not deny water baptism to those who spoke in other languages as they had. Remember water baptism is an action that testifies to the fact that something has happened. Being baptized without the commitment to the Christian life will not gain you any points in Heaven.

# Water Baptism

### Can You Be Saved Without Being Baptized?

When Jesus was hanging on the cross just before His death, He took the time to grant eternal life to one of the thieves hanging beside Him. When the thief asked Jesus to remember him when He came into His kingdom, Jesus responded by telling him that he would indeed be with Him in paradise before the day was over. Since they were both hanging on crosses at the time and didn't get down before they died, the thief was never baptized. Was he granted eternal life? According to the Bible he was. If by some change of circumstance he would have been pardoned and let down from the cross, he no doubt would have been baptized. The overwhelming example of conversions in Scripture was that when the decision was made, baptism followed.

Once you have made your own personal decision to follow Jesus Christ, I encourage you to make your decision known publicly just as they did in the Bible. Let your pastor know that you want to be obedient to the commandment Jesus gave His disciples to be baptized in water. Say to all present that you are beginning a new life.

### Discussion Points:
1. What is baptism?
2. Who should be baptized?
3. Do you have to be baptized to be saved?
4. If Jesus never sinned, why was He baptized?

### Memory Verse:

**Go ye therefore, and teach all nations, baptizing them in the name of the Father, and of the Son, and of the Holy Ghost.**

**Teaching them to observe all things whatsoever I have commanded you: and, lo, I am with you alway, even unto the end of the world. Amen.**

**Matthew 28:19,20**

# Lesson #7
# Faith Toward God

Faith is perhaps one of the most discussed and debated subjects in Christianity. Some people feel that their personal belief about something guarantees the delivery of the thing for which they are wishing. People find a verse in the Scriptures that seems to address their situation, and then they attempt to hold God hostage to an isolated promise to the exclusion of the wisdom of the rest of the Scriptures. Having faith does not mean that you have discovered the secret of getting God to do what you want Him to do. It does mean, however, that you have discovered the joy of trusting Him with the affairs of your life, even when you don't understand why some things happen the way they do.

It is easy to feel confident about life when everything is going well. You could easily draw the wrong conclusion that your life is blessed because you are trying hard to do the right thing. God perhaps has created you for better things than others will get to enjoy in life. You are special. All of these and other similar lines of thinking may well lead you down a dangerous path. If you conclude that your goodness or your feeling of being special are somehow responsible for your blessings, then you will also be forced to assume that, when difficult times come, you must be lacking in some way so as to have caused your difficulties.

Remember, faith is not some magic potion you obtain and then pull out to use to solve your problems. Sometimes people tend to impose their own wishful thinking or selfish desires on situations and assume God will back them up and do whatever they want. When things don't conform to your preconceived notions, it is easy to get your feelings hurt and feel that God has let you down. Getting God to bless your plan is not what faith is all about. Faith is, however, the result of a life relationship whereby you get to know the God of heaven and come to trust that He has a plan for your life and is working to bring His plan into being. You also come to understand that, even though it may not look like it at the moment, His plan is a good one and will eventually work out for your good.

Do you remember the first time you flew on an airplane? If your experience was similar to mine, you saw airplanes fly long before you actually got on one. In my case, I had heard that they could fly. I had spoken to people who had been on them. I had seen them far overhead as they raced from one place to another. As I processed all that information, I came to a mental belief that flying was indeed possible. But the first time I actually strapped on the seat belt and prepared to take my first flight, all of that mental belief was challenged. At that moment I was forced to see if I really believed airplanes could fly. My heart raced as we roared down the runway and the plane eventually lifted into the air. That was thirty-one years ago. Since then I have flown more times than I can count. It still takes faith to get on a plane and trust my well being to someone else. Today, however, I am more comfortable with my "flying faith" because I have more experience.

The Scriptures say that faith comes by hearing, and hearing by the Word of God. If you want to mature to a more comfortable faith, the secret is to have more experience with God. You see, God wants you to get to know and trust Him. Don't trade getting to know *about* God for getting to know *Him*. You can hear all the testimonies in the world and still be disappointed when you try to get God to respond on your behalf. The secret to faith is to hear from God for your own self. You will find that when your insides hear Heaven's instructions, those instructions also come with a conviction that what you heard is possible and will come to pass. When God speaks and you hear, it becomes very difficult to turn your back and walk away. The difficult part is hearing clearly enough to know without a doubt that what you heard was indeed from Heaven. So how do you hear?

There are many ways to hear from God. You may be listening to a Christian radio or television program and suddenly the words seem to come alive. Or, as you are praying, a thought may be strongly impressed on your mind. In a church service it may seem that the pastor is speaking directly to you. The Bible says that faith comes by hearing and hearing by the Word of God. The safest way to be sure that what you are hearing is acceptable to build your faith on is to be sure that it does not contradict what is already written in the Scriptures.

God has instituted a wonderfully secure plan to help you keep on track while you are on this journey to live a life acceptable to Him. While there are many ways to hear a word from God, no word or message from God will oppose the truths already recorded in the Scriptures. If God simply changed His will or the rules by which He wanted you to live whenever He wanted to, it would be impossible to ever live with confidence that you were doing the right thing. It is difficult enough to get it right with one set of standards. Imagine trying to please someone who changed the rules all the time.

You may not always like what you find in the Scriptures, but one thing is certain. God's Word can be counted on and trusted to eventually lead you to a fulfilled life. When you were created, God had a plan for your life. The challenge is for you to find that plan and give yourself in partnership with God to complete the task for which you were created. Knowing this to be true, you may wonder, "How do the words of the Bible produce in me the faith to live the way God intends me to live?"

When Jesus had completed His work on earth, and was ready to return to heaven, He gave His disciples a wonderful gift. He said that they would not be left alone after He returned to His Father. His plan was to send the Holy Spirit to be with them after He left. (To find out more about the Holy Spirit and the Spirit-filled life, refer to Lesson #13.) The Holy Spirit serves a valuable and unique role in the life of the believer. One of His primary roles is to interpret the truths of the Scriptures to the heart of the believer. You see, hearing with your ears alone is not enough to build your faith. The Holy Spirit's job is to help your heart hear the Word of God in such a way as to be believed.

You may hear the same truths repeatedly and not understand them but then, one day, everything seems to make sense. Something inside you says, "I believe that." The greatest struggle is not to hear physically, but to hear in your heart in such a way as to be convinced that what you have heard is indeed the truth. Once you cross the barrier to the place where you hear the Word in your heart and believe what you have heard, faith is the result.

Something quite wonderful happens as real faith is born in the human heart. The previous struggle to find a way to believe is replaced with a confident knowing that refuses to be denied. Once you come to that place, you will find that you have begun a journey that has many signposts of confirmation after reconfirmation that God indeed does watch over His Word to perform it. You see, you will always do what you believe. It is the believing that is the hard part. Once you believe, acting on what you believe gets easier and easier. Let me give you an example.

The Scriptures teach us that we should tithe on our increase and we will be blessed if we do. Preachers try to convince us that tithing is the way to financial success. We hear testimonies of others who tithe and are blessed for their obedience. From all the evidence we begin to have this feeling down inside that there may be something to all this and we make an attempt to get in on the good deal. After a week or two, however, things aren't going so well, and we begin to wonder if this plan will work for us.

Our hope (not yet faith) was that somehow this thing called tithing would start to work right away and we would be better off financially. When it doesn't work quickly, our resolve weakens and we back off on our commitment. What was begun as a search for financial blessing is now the source of frustration and guilt. Not only are we not blessed, but we also feel guilty for not being obedient. Our mind wrestles with the contradiction in which we find ourselves.

Whether it is tithing, witnessing, praying or any number of other Christian truths, you can find yourself in the no-man's land of having tried and failed to incorporate these truths into your daily life. If, however, you fellowship with the Holy Spirit about your dilemma, at some point you will find a miraculous difference.

Remember that His job is to lead you into the truth about the thing you are trying to understand. When the Holy Spirit teaches your inner man about tithing or any other spiritual truth, you become convinced in such a way that any other action except obedience becomes unthinkable. At that point you are no longer testing the tithing thing to see if you can get blessed, you are tithing because you are simply acting on what you believe.

In the final analysis faith is quite simple once you acquire it in an area of your life. With the help of the Holy Spirit you become completely convinced that what He has told you is the truth. From that point forward you are simply acting on what you believe. If someone told you the building you are in was on fire, it wouldn't take long to figure out what you believe about what you were told. If you believed it was on fire, you would quickly get out of the building. If you didn't believe the building was on fire, you would probably stay put. You see, it is easy to find out what you believe. Just look at the choices you make. Watch what you do and you will see what you believe.

If you don't like what your life is producing from your belief system, then expose yourself to God's Word and open yourself to the Holy Spirit. As you fellowship with God, His opinions will rub off on you and you will find you will begin to change in positive ways. The result of these changes starts to build a track record of success. The further you go down the road of obedience, the more convinced you become that God's way is indeed the right way.

This may seem to be a slow process in the beginning, but once you see God answer your prayer or come to your financial rescue, you begin to understand God's commitment to His Word. The longer you walk with

*Faith Toward God*

Him, the more evidence you find that you indeed can trust Him. This trust is the essence of a life commitment to God and His kingdom. It is from this trust that you will eventually develop a faith toward God that gives Him the benefit of the doubt. When you face problems for which you have no answers, you will still find the confidence to say, "God I trust you to take this impossible situation and cause something good to result from it." When you arrive at that place of trust, you have faith toward God.

*Discussion Points:*

1. What is the difference in hearing with your ears and hearing with your heart?

2. What is the Holy Spirit's role in developing your faith?

3. What does action have to do with believing?

4. How can you learn to trust God?

*Memory Verse:*

**So then faith cometh by hearing, and hearing by the word of God.**

**Romans 10:17**

## Lesson #8
# Kings and Priests

Now that you have made your decision to live the Christian life, you will want to find your place of service in the family of God. The wonderful thing about being part of a family is that there are many different roles required to complete the family tree. In this family everybody has a vital role to fulfill. Sitting on the sidelines is not an option.

*Romans 12:1* says it this way:

**"I beseech you therefore, brethren, by the mercies of God, that ye present your bodies a living sacrifice, holy, acceptable unto God, which is your reasonable service."**

Usually the first thing that comes to mind when someone reads that verse is that we are going to be required to serve God in some remote jungle until we die all alone by some horrible disease. While there are those who are chosen to serve God as apostles, prophets, evangelists, pastors and teachers, it goes without saying that it is not possible for all Christians to serve in only those five roles. Yet all of us are called to serve.

There is an interesting division of responsibilities in the Old Testament that offers some valuable insight into other options of service. When God set up the social and spiritual structure of Israel, He established two distinct and different offices to keep the nation balanced: the office of the priest and the office of the king. The priest was primarily responsible for the spiritual life of the nation, while the king was primarily responsible for social order and the national defense. The priest ministered to God in teaching the law and ceremonial worship. The king ministered to God by warring with the enemies of Israel and protecting Israel from the destructive forces of Godless cultures.

At the end of the day the priest would go back to the temple, and the king would return to the palace. When things were going well, the two rarely interfered with each other's business. When there was a challenge from a neighboring enemy, the priest would hear from God and tell the king how Heaven wanted to address the problem. The king would respond according to the way he was instructed. Usually he would beat up the bad guys and take their stuff. He would then return with the spoils of war and offer them to God in the presence of the priest. The priest would then use the provision to meet the needs of the less fortunate.

I know this is an oversimplified example, but one thing can't be denied. When both of these offices worked according to the plan laid out in the Scriptures, the nation of Israel prospered. In fact, things worked so well in Israel that the Israelites were the envy of the nations around them. Wouldn't it be a wonderful testimony of the modern church if the same were said of us? I believe there is a way the favor of God can rest upon the Church today, much in the same way as it rested upon Israel.

> "And hath made us kings and priests unto God and his Father; to him be glory and dominion for ever and ever. Amen."
>
> **Revelation 1:6**

Remember, if everybody were called to be a priest, there wouldn't be anybody left for the priests to serve. In Israel the priesthood was a relatively small part of the nation. In fact, when you research the numbers, you will find that only one in twenty-seven men were priests. If all believers are called to serve God and only one in twenty-seven are called to the priesthood, what are the rest of us to do? The rest serve on the king's side of the Kingdom. The working, building, warring, educating, governing, commerce side of the Kingdom falls to the rest of us.

While it is true that those who serve God in spiritual ministry have specific gifts and anointings, they are no more full-time or gifted than you are. As a believer in Jesus Christ, you have committed your life to serve Him. The only difference in your calling and the calling of a pastor is where and how you serve.

You see, the pastors and other staff workers in the local church have been called by God to train and equip you, the Church, to do the work of the ministry out in the marketplace. No matter how good or anointed your church staff is, it is only one in twenty-seven and can never reach the whole world by itself.

**"And he gave some, apostles; and some, prophets; and some, evangelists; and some, pastors and teachers;**

**For the perfecting of the saints, for the work of the ministry, for the edifying of the body of Christ."**

**Ephesians 4:11,12**

The real work of expanding the Kingdom of God on planet earth is to be done by all those who believe. God's plan was never to have the saints hire someone to go into all the world for them. We are all called and blessed to be a part of spreading this Good News to the whole world.

"Go ye therefore, and teach all nations, baptizing them in the name of the Father, and of the Son, and of the Holy Ghost."

Matthew 28:19

When an evangelist or pastor preaches the Gospel that God loves mankind so much that He sent His Son Jesus to die for the sins of all, people will respond to the truth they hear. The challenge is to come back a year later and see how many of those who made the decision to become a Christian are still faithful to their decision. Have you ever wondered why so many make the right decision, but for some reason, don't follow through?

Jesus told His disciples a story beginning in *Luke 8:5* about a farmer that explains this problem perfectly. This farmer scattered his seed on four different kinds of ground. Some fell by the wayside but never took root. Other seed fell on stony ground, some among thorns and some fell on good soil. While all of the last three took root, only the seed in the good soil ever bore fruit. If you had been the farmer, you would have seen three out of every four seeds sown spring up, but, when it came time for the harvest, you would have seen only one out of four actually bear fruit.

How disappointing to have done all that work, thinking you would reap a great harvest, only to get a return on one-fourth of your seed. In our lives, I believe the reason more seed doesn't produce fruit is that the culture of this world chokes the life out of the decisions made when the Gospel is first believed. Many people hear and believe (receive) the seed of God's Word. Before long, however, factors such as the routine of daily life, friends, work environment, families, hobbies, movies and music begin to water down the purity of the commitment they once made to Christ. Culture is the strongest pull on our lives. If the culture issue is not properly addressed, it will steal one-half of the seed.

How does this apply to you? From our discussion above you discovered that most people are called to the king's side of service in the Kingdom. Kings work with twenty-seven times more people than the church staff does. You are out there in the culture and marketplace every day. When you bring Godly influence to the place in which you live and work, there is a much greater chance that the decisions made for righteousness' sake will not be forgotten in the busyness of life. By creating a righteous environment in the marketplace and the home, the one-half of the seed lost to the cares of life in *Luke 8* can be salvaged and made fruitful.

The Christian who is committed to living out the Christian life in society brings the cause of Christ to the front lines by confronting the war against darkness right where it is happening. Most real sinners may never meet a Christian's pastor, but they might work with the Christian every day. When there are more believers at one's work than there are non-believers, there is the subtle pressure to conform to righteousness. The world has had the upper hand in the marketplace too long. When believers take their stand, it is possible to change the culture of the world in which they live.

How can you bring Christ into your workplace? As a businessperson, offer what you have to God for His use. Ask Him to use your gifts, talents and resources to further His Kingdom on earth. Something as insignificant as the little boy's loaves and fishes can become a great blessing to many when put into the Master's hands. Those who train the young, care for the sick, make movies, create businesses, report the news, write songs or perform other such jobs are those who hold the power in society. Use what you have and see the Kingdom come on earth as it is in Heaven.

*Discussion Points:*

1. Are all Christians called to serve?

2. How were the roles of the kings and priests different in the Old Testament?

3. What role does culture play in the life of the believer?

4. What do you have to offer to God for Him to use?

*Memory Verse:*

**I beseech you therefore, brethren, by the mercies of God, that ye present your bodies a living sacrifice, holy, acceptable unto God, which is your reasonable service.**

**Romans 12:1**

# LESSON #9
# Eternal Judgment

One of the basic, fundamental doctrines of the Church listed in *Hebrews 6:2* is that of eternal judgment. Both of those words are quite serious. Linking the words eternity and judgment together creates an "Oh no! What did I do?" feeling about the subject. By the time we are finished, however, I hope you will see that, as always, God has something good in mind for those who love Him.

Judgment is a difficult subject to approach because most of us do not want to think about the possibility that we may have to be accountable to someone for the actions of our lives. It is threatening enough to consider that we will stand before God; but to stand there and have all our deep, dark secrets revealed, and then have to answer to Him for our actions and thoughts is simply more than we can deal with. How can we ever find peace in our lives if there is the continual reminder that, not only have we failed, but also we will probably continue to fail?

### *Guilt*

The guilt that comes from the constant reminder that we somehow don't measure up has a very simple explanation. When we fail to perform at the level expected of us, the shortcoming is expressed in our emotions as *guilt*.

Some examples include the following: If we were supposed to have picked someone up at four o'clock and didn't arrive until five, we let that person down. If we had studied harder for a test, we wouldn't have gotten that "C." If we hadn't said that awful thing to a friend, we wouldn't have hurt his feelings. The result in each case was that, afterwards, we felt guilty.

Life is full of shortcomings that result in hurts, disappointments and a whole myriad of emotions. The crushing weight of guilt distorts values, relationships and the potential that God created in all of us. Satan's plan is to use guilt to disqualify us from our God-ordained task of serving others in this world.

There are only two ways to live life in such a way as not to produce feelings of guilt. We either have to raise our performance or lower our unattainable expectations. Raising performance is a difficult task. It can be done, but it isn't easy. We may try to stop smoking, lose twenty pounds or think only pure thoughts about others by simply deciding that we should. If it were as easy as making a decision, the weight loss industry in America wouldn't be an eight billion-dollar a year business. Changing is not so easy. When we try as hard as we possibly can and still fail, it is devastating to our self-image. When the picture we carry inside ourselves isn't a pretty one, it is difficult to find any hope that things will ever be different.

This sense of coming up short is the essence of sin. The Scriptures say that we all have sinned and come short of the glory of God. If we can't raise our performance, and we don't see any way to lower what is expected of us, the life we live will only be filled with disappointments and guilt. To make things even worse, the Bible tells us that the wages (fair and just payment) of sin equal death. We try and try to get it right, but still fail. For all of our effort to reform ourselves, we still must give an account to God for our shortcomings.

Is it any wonder that so many people find life so difficult? It appears that there is no way to win. The requirements for a peaceful, happy life seem out of reach. If this were the end of the story, we would all find the nearest bridge and jump off. The truth is that man was born into a system that is flawed. When Adam lost his dominion to Satan, the peace in which God intended for man to live was lost. It is Satan that exploits our feelings of failure and guilt to create a hopeless future.

### *What Is the Answer to Our Problem?*

When God sent Jesus into this world to die as the payment for our shortcomings (sins), He had more in mind than just extending to us a pardon for our offenses. Yes, He forgives, but He also offers us a whole new standard by which we can live. Jesus also came to clearly define God's expectations. Knowing what God expects of us is the secret to guilt-free living. Remember, if what God expected of us were not possible, then He would have no right to judge us.

How, then, can you live up to God's expectations? First, read your Bible and study it to find what God requires of you. Then ask Him for the power to live the life you find revealed in the Scriptures. God does have standards, and He expects you to live by them. As a Christian, you can now *anticipate* God's help and also *depend on* His help to live a life pleasing to Him. You will see that, as you find God's will and with His help do it, you will not only live guilt-free, but you will also get to know God as a friend. After all, it is the restoration of your relationship with God that was the reason for Jesus' coming to the earth. He came to earth to redeem you from the curse of coming up short in your service to God.

When you find that it is indeed possible to live a life pleasing to God and you actually begin to live that life, you will also find the fulfillment which causes life to make sense. Life will no longer be filled with the dread of someday facing a Judge that you could never please. Instead, life will then be a wonderful journey that leads you to a reunion with the God who brings true meaning and hope for your future.

For all of you there will come the time when you must present yourself before God to find out your eternal dwelling place. His judgment will be completely fair and completely final. There will be no purgatory of second chances. When that day arrives, the criteria of judgment will not be whether or not you lived a perfect life, but whether or not you accepted the perfect gift. God's gift of eternal life is offered to all who believe and accept it. Whatever you do in this life, be sure that you are properly prepared to face God's judgment that begins your eternity.

*Everybody Exists Forever.*

The truth is that everybody will exist forever. The sad truth is that, while those who have properly prepared to meet their God will enter into Heaven, those who have not prepared for judgment will exist forever away from the presence of God in punishment. Yes, Heaven and hell are both real places that will be the final destination of all mankind. Heaven is the place of eternal life in the presence of God, while hell is the place of eternal death and separation from God. Just being separated from all that is good and holy would be bad enough, but hell is also a place of torment.

Some religions incorrectly teach that people will have a second chance to make their peace with God after they leave this life. No, we don't get to come back to earth and try again either. The Scriptures don't support these false teachings. The Bible says that it is appointed unto man once to die and after that comes the judgment. *Revelation 22:11* tells us to let the just be just still and the wicked be wicked still. In other words, once God has made His judgment, there will be no way to change His decision. The time to determine eternal destination is *now*, in *this* life.

Because you were born into this world of sin with the need to be reconciled to God, your first response to judgment may be to try to avoid it. It is important that you begin to think differently about your standing before God in order to find fulfillment in this life and to be fully prepared for the next.

Suppose you were notified that a relative had died and left you a large tract of land worth millions of dollars. You were also notified that another relative had claimed ownership of the same property. In order to take possession of the land, you were ordered to appear before a judge, due to the challenge to your ownership. The judge you were to appear before was going to issue a judgment as to the true owner of the property. Would you avoid the court, fearing that your claim would be denied; or would you arrive full of confidence, knowing that the truth would be upheld and you would be awarded what was rightfully yours?

While you did nothing to earn or deserve the ownership of the property, if it was legally given to you, you would expect to be declared the rightful owner. In the same manner, all judgment isn't to be dreaded. Even though you and I don't deserve the gift of eternal life, it is still offered to us through faith in the death and resurrection of Jesus Christ. The fact that you and I are not worthy of such a gift has nothing to do with our legal standing, once we accept Heaven's generosity.

Eternal judgment is based solely on whether or not we accept the death of Jesus Christ as payment in full for our sins. God has already said that He accepts Jesus' death as payment in full to meet all requirements for our entrance into Heaven. He cannot award in our favor, however, unless we agree to the terms of the offer. By accepting Jesus Christ as our Lord and Savior and determining to live a life pleasing to Him, our names are written in the *Book of Eternal Life*. If we do agree, we are then judged eternally blessed and forgiven.

## What Are the Terms?

Someday this life will be over for all of us. On that day we will all stand before God and be judged on how we lived our lives. Isn't it nice to know we can be fully prepared to face that day with joy and excitement? When judgment comes, we won't have to defend ourselves. We will be able to confidently rely on His mercy and grace.

> **"For we ourselves also were sometimes foolish, disobedient, deceived, serving divers lusts and pleasures, living in malice and envy, hateful, and hating one another.**
>
> **"But after that the kindness and love of God our Savior toward man appeared,**
>
> **Not by works of righteousness which we have done, but according to His mercy He saved us, by the washing of regeneration, and renewing of the Holy Ghost;**
>
> **which He shed on us abundantly through Jesus Christ our Savior;**
>
> **that being justified by His grace, we should be made heirs according to the hope of eternal life."**
>
> **Titus 3:3-7**

*Eternal Judgment*

## *What Should You Do?*

Once you have found your own peace with God, you will find a genuine desire to share what you have found with others. There is no greater gift you can give to the people of the world, caught in the same destructive cycle of sin you have just escaped, than to help them find their own relationship with God. When you recognize the hurt in others that used to be in you, take the risk to introduce them to the God who can give meaning to this life and offer hope for the life to come.

### *Discussion Points:*

1. How can judgment be good?
2. What is the basis for our eternal judgment?
3. Will anyone get a second chance after death?
4. After we find peace with God, what should we do?

### *Memory Verse:*

**And as it is appointed unto men once to die, but after this the judgment.**

**Hebrews 9:27**

# Lesson #10
# Scripture Reading

Perhaps one of the most remarkable truths of the Christian faith is the fact that God didn't leave us here to figure out this life all by ourselves. First, God has given us the Bible, and then He sent the Holy Spirit to live inside us to help us understand it. God put great effort into providing us with a written standard by which we are to live our lives and a teacher to help us apply the Scriptures correctly. As we become more familiar with the Bible, we find that it contains instruction concerning every aspect of our lives.

## Principle #1 — The Bible is the Word of God.

*"For the prophecy came not in old time by the will of man: but holy men of God spake as they were moved by the Holy Ghost."* **1 Peter 1:21**

How did God deliver this most unusual book to mankind? The Bible says that the Holy Spirit inspired men to write the Scriptures. That means that God told men what He wanted to say and they wrote it down. The Bible makes an astounding claim that sets it apart from any other book ever written. Because God authored the Bible, it is literally the Word of God. How wonderful to be able to live your life having the resource of God's counsel available for any situation that you may face!

The challenge in the early part of your Christian journey is to find out whether you can really trust the teachings of the Scriptures as a foundation upon which to build your life. There is a simple way to prove for yourself if the writings of the Scriptures can indeed be elevated to that of an infallible, divine message. Begin to live by the principles outlined in the Scriptures, and you will soon discover that they really are true.

In the book of John, Jesus promised blessing for those who keep His commandments. You see, God didn't give us the Scriptures just to show us how wise He is. His Word was also intended to show us how we can live a successful life. The Bible teaches us the principles to live by and gives us the promises and blessings that accompany Biblical living.

## Principle #2 — Study the Bible; don't just read it.

**"Study to shew thyself approved unto God, a workman that needeth not to be ashamed, rightly dividing the word of truth."**
**2 Timothy 2:15**

There is nothing magical about holding the Bible or sleeping with it under your pillow. Reading and quoting the Scriptures are a step in the right direction. The best relationship you can have with the Scriptures, however, is to seek to understand what the Bible says and then live your life by the principles you find. When the Word of God is believed and acted upon, the power of the Scriptures is released in the life of the believer.

**"So shall My word be that goeth forth out of my mouth: it shall not return unto me void, but it shall accomplish that which I please, and it shall prosper in the thing whereto I sent it."**
**Isaiah 55:11**

## Scripture Reading

God's Word is true, and you will find it can therefore be trusted. Although your circumstances may not immediately line up with the Scriptures, you will find that once you begin to live by its guidelines, your life will start to change. The word *accomplish* in the passage above indicates "a process of time." Knowing the Scriptures is not like pushing a magic button that fixes everything. Gaining understanding of the Word is, however, a reliable foundation of truth upon which you can build a successful life.

The Bible likens the Word of God to a seed that is sown in the heart of man. When you plant a seed, you don't expect the harvest the same day. It takes time for the seed to grow into a plant that produces fruit. It is the same when you discover a truth in the Scriptures and decide to put it into practice. You take God's Word inside yourself by reading, believing and then acting upon what you believe. This process is called *faith*. You have no evidence other than the promises you have found in the Scriptures, but you begin to act in accordance with the truth you have found.

**"So then faith cometh by hearing, and hearing by the word of God."**
**Romans 10:17**

In time, as this process continues, you will find yourself beginning to trust in and rely more and more on the Bible as the standard for the way you live your life. As you prove one truth to yourself, the next one will seem easier to believe. Hearing God speak to your heart will give you the courage to live a life pleasing to Him. The safest way to hear that still small voice is to read the Bible and ask the Holy Spirit to help you understand what you are reading. Whatever else you hear, always make sure that it is in agreement with the standard of the written Scriptures and you will never get off track.

*Second Timothy 3:16,17* says it this way:

"All Scripture is given by inspiration of God, and is profitable for doctrine, for reproof, for correction, for instruction in righteousness:

That the man of God may be perfect, thoroughly furnished unto all good works."

## Principle #3 — Get a plan.

One thing is for sure: if you don't begin reading the Bible, you will find it very difficult to get to know God. There are many different ways to read your Bible. When you first begin, you may find it helpful to read the books of Genesis and John. These two books capture the essence of God's nature perhaps better than any other two books in the Bible. After all, it is God about whom you want to know.

Next, find a plan that will expose you to the entire book. Don't be intimidated by the size of the Bible. You have a lifetime to discover the wonders it contains. I find it helpful to read until the Holy Spirit teaches me something I didn't know before, and then I think about that truth until it is accepted into my internal belief system. You may come up with something completely different but, whatever you do, expose yourself to God's Word everyday. Listen to the Bible on a CD while you are in your car. Read every morning before you start your day. Read before bed if you are a night person. Just be sure that somehow you do it everyday.

## Principle #4 — God's Word will keep you on track.

Growing to maturity as a Christian is a wonderful road of self-discovery. You will find that as you learn more about God, you will begin to change. It is impossible to love God and read His word and remain the same person as you were before. You will also find that you will like the new you better than the old you. The standards for living revealed in the Scriptures are simply a better way to live. After all, since it was God who created man in the beginning, it only makes sense that He would also hold the secrets to living a successful and fulfilled life.

Living the Christian life is really quite simple. I didn't say it was easy, but it is simple. If you read your Bible and do what it says, you will find fulfillment. You will never be at odds with God if you simply do what His Word says. You will find there all the direction you need to be pleasing to your God.

"Thy word is a lamp unto my feet, and a light unto my path." **Psalm 119:105**

*Discussion Points:*

1. Is the Bible really the Word of God?
2. Why should you study your Bible?
3. How is the Word of God like a seed?
4. What is your plan to regularly read and study the Bible?
5. How does the Bible keep me from sin?

*Memory Verses:*

**Thy word have I hid in mine heart, that I might not sin against thee. Psalm 119:11**

**For whatsoever things were written aforetime were written for our learning, that we through patience and comfort of the Scriptures might have hope. Romans 15:4**

# Lesson #11
# Resurrection of the Dead

The one inescapable fact of life is that someday this life will be over for all of us. Since the day Satan lied to Adam and Eve in the Garden of Eden, telling them that they would not die for disobeying God, we have sought an answer to the question of what will happen to us after death. Every major religion tries to address the issue. The answers offered range from "oblivion" to "second chances" to "everybody wins." The wondrous truth of the Christian faith is that the eternity promised to believers is backed up by an unprecedented event that validates the hope for the life to come.

Jesus came to earth with the full intention of dying for the sins of the world and then rising from the dead. This was not a near death experience in which the victim was revived to live a natural life for awhile then die again. The coming back to life that Jesus experienced was called a *resurrection*. This resurrection is the single most significant event in the history of the world.

Jesus told His disciples over and over that He was going to be put to death and then rise to life again. It was difficult for them to fully comprehend what Jesus was saying since they had never seen anyone resurrected. They had seen people come back from the dead in Jesus' ministry. Resurrection is different. In fact, when Jesus was finally crucified and had fulfilled His destiny as the Savior of the world, the disciples were so overcome with grief that they completely forgot Jesus had told them He was going to be resurrected. They were more concerned with their own safety and, thus, hid out in a locked room for fear that the authorities would come to arrest them.

This fear of death is so strong in mankind that it can keep you from hearing what God has to say to you, too. Remember, it was God's plan from the beginning that man would live forever. Death only came into the world through sin. Part of God's plan to bring you back into fellowship with Him will, over time, begin to deal with this universal fear of what is waiting for you after this life. As you get to know God and begin to understand His plan, you will see that He still wants you to live forever. He has determined to work with you throughout your life to prepare you for the day you stand before Him.

The defining moment in history that made restoration with God possible was the moment Jesus rose from the dead. Jesus, who was blameless, took upon Himself the sins of the world and entered hell. Because He was blameless, death had no right to hold Him. He was declared innocent and, therefore, the prison of death and the power of dying had to release Him. That meant He would not only come back from the dead, but He would also come back in a body that couldn't age, decay or ever die.

> "Whom God hath raised up, having loosed the pains of death: because it was not possible that He should be holden of it."
> **Acts 2:24**

The body Jesus had when He rose from the dead was no longer like the one He had lived in for the thirty-three years He was on the earth. While the disciples were locked in that room, fearing for their lives, Jesus suddenly appeared by passing through a locked door. The disciples thought He was a spirit.

> "Behold My hands and My feet, that it is I myself: handle Me, and see; for a spirit hath not flesh and bones, as ye see Me have.
>
> And when He had thus spoken, He shewed them His hands and His feet.
>
> And while they yet believed not for joy, and wondered, He said unto them, Have ye here any meat?
>
> And they gave Him a piece of a broiled fish, and of an honeycomb.
>
> And He took it, and did eat before them."
>
> Luke 24:39-43

It is interesting to note that Jesus told His disciples His new body was flesh and bone (made of tangible substances). However, although Jesus was able to eat fish and honey with them, he could also appear and disappear. It is clear that, in order to live for eternity in the spiritual world, we need the kind of body that will never be subject to the power of death.

The glorious hope of the salvation message is that we are able to benefit from the resurrection power that raised Jesus from the dead. The *power of the Holy Spirit indwelling the believer* is that power.

> "But if the Spirit of Him that raised up Jesus from the dead dwell in you, He that raised up Christ from the dead shall also quicken your mortal bodies by His Spirit that dwelleth in you."
>
> Romans 8:11

One historical fact is undeniable: Jesus is the only spiritual leader in all of history who ever came back from the dead in an eternal spiritual body. If you were to open Mohammed's, Buddha's and Confucius' graves, what would you find? You would find their bones because they never were touched by resurrection power. You don't have to open Jesus' grave. Angels opened it on the third day after His burial. His bones are not there because He is risen.

What else but the resurrection could explain the miraculous turnaround in the attitudes of His disciples? They were transformed from a fearful group, huddled in a locked room, into a radical army that could not be silenced in their proclamation of the fact that Jesus was risen. Peter went from denying Christ before the crucifixion, to preaching the resurrection of Jesus in the temple, after He had appeared to them in that locked room. The disciples were so permanently affected by Jesus' resurrection that they remained true to their story even unto their own deaths.

Even the religious leaders who were responsible for Jesus' death were convinced that He really did come back from the dead. They were so concerned about what would happen when His disciples found out, they paid off the soldiers who were guarding the tomb and made up a story that the disciples had stolen His body. If they had stolen His body in an attempt to rally the troops, why were they hiding and then later willing to die believing their own lie? The only explanation for the empty tomb, the boldness of the disciples and the fear of the religious leaders is that Jesus did indeed rise from the dead.

> **"And when they were assembled with the elders, and had taken counsel, they gave large money unto the soldiers,**
>
> **Saying, Say ye, His disciples came by night, and stole him away while we slept.**

And if this come to the governor's ears, we will persuade him, and secure you.

So they took the money, and did as they were taught: and this saying is commonly reported among the Jews until this day.
Matthew 28:12-15

The Scriptures further reveal that, one day, this life will not only be over for those who have believed in Jesus, but it also will come to a defining moment for all mankind. Jesus will return once again to be reunited with His Church that is alive on earth. At His return the power of the resurrection will be released upon all those who believe. The righteous dead will be resurrected with a new and different body that is eternal, and those who are the living Church on earth will be changed. When that day comes, we will have no regrets about whatever price we paid to stay qualified for the resurrection of those who have been justified by their belief in Jesus Christ.

"Behold, I shew you a mystery; We shall not all sleep (die), but we shall all be changed,

In a moment, in the twinkling of an eye, at the last trump: for the trumpet shall sound, and the dead shall be raised incorruptible, and we shall be changed.

For this corruptible must put on incorruption, and this mortal must put on immortality.

So when this corruptible shall have put on incorruption, and this mortal shall have put on immortality, then shall be brought to pass the saying that is written, Death is swallowed up in victory."
1 Corinthians 15:51-54

*Discussion Points:*

1. How is resurrection different from simply having a near death experience?

2. What sets Jesus' life apart from the lives of other spiritual leaders?

3. How did the change in the behavior of the disciples seem to confirm the resurrection?

4. What is the resurrection of the just?

*Memory Verse:*

**But if the Spirit of Him that raised up Jesus from the dead dwell in you, He that raised up Christ from the dead shall also quicken your mortal bodies by His Spirit that dwelleth in you.**

**Romans 8:11**

# Lesson #12
# Fellowship

Have you ever noticed how people tend to pick up the traits of the group with which they spend the most time? The next time you are in a place where groups of people are gathered, look around and see if it isn't true. One group will all be wearing black. In another all will have tattoos. Two girls walking together will have on the same jacket. In every society, under the misguided idea that we all want to be individuals, we tend to make choices that bring us into conformity with the group whose approval we seek.

## Principle #1 — Social pressure is powerful.

This social pressure, whether subtle or overt, has more to do with how we live our lives than we might care to admit. Every subculture in a society has its own language, dress code, code of conduct and belief system. How many have stood on the fringes of a social group, vowing that it would not change them, only to look up sometime later and find that there is little difference between themselves and the rest of the group? Herein lies the power of the drug culture, religious cults, political movements, motorcycle gangs, environmental groups and any other culture that requires strong opinions to stay in the group.

**"And be not conformed to this world: but be ye transformed by the renewing of your mind, that ye**

may prove what is that good, and acceptable, and perfect, will of God."

Romans 12:2

This power can be used for either good or evil. The fact that social groups exert pressure to conform will require you to examine your social life if you are serious about living victoriously in Christ. You will find that one of the first and most obvious evidences of whether your decision to follow Christ was real is that there will be friction between your new Christian friends and your old group. Often the old group will not be all that excited about this new life you have found. As much as you may want to tell those in the old group about your new life in Christ, they may not want to listen.

"Be ye not unequally yoked together with unbelievers: for what fellowship hath righteousness with unrighteousness? and what communion hath light with darkness?"

2 Corinthians 6:14

This rejection by your old friends is often confusing and painful. It seems the more serious you are about a sincere effort to help them understand your decision to be a Christian, the more they withdraw and ridicule your decision. You are now a challenge to the culture of the group and, therefore, you should expect to be shunned. As difficult as it is at the time, you simply must understand that you will live through the rejection, and your life will find order again.

Even if the old life was sinful and wrong, it was predictable. This predictability was comfortable and, now that it is changing, you will feel out of place and uncomfortable for a while. During this transitional season in which you are putting off the old culture and putting on the new one, you may find yourself questioning the wisdom of your decision. Don't be discouraged. Your new life will soon begin to feel right and normal, and returning to the old way of living will become repulsive. Knowing that these feelings are a normal part of the process of becoming a new creation in Christ will help you through the awkwardness and into a new way of living.

Your desire to help your old friends find what you have found may or may not be successful in bringing them to the Kingdom of God. One thing is for sure, however, if you don't change them, and you continue to spend large amounts of time with them, there is a strong chance that they will change you. You must ask yourself if their friendship is worth risking your eternity.

**"He that walketh with wise men shall be wise: but a companion of fools shall be destroyed."**

**Proverbs 13:20**

## Principle #2 — Fellowship with the right group.

Fellowship is a word used in this context to refer to a group of people sharing common interests or purpose. If you really want to catch onto something, hang around with people who know more about the subject than you do. By watching them, talking with them and just being with them, you will find that what they have begins to become yours. This environmental immersion will allow you to absorb the information much faster than if you were locked away to study by yourself. The most effective way to learn a foreign language is to immerse yourself in a culture in which the language is spoken. The same is true when you are in the early stages of your faith.

As a new believer, it is essential that you learn the basics of your faith as soon as possible. That is one of the reasons for this material. When a plant is young and tender, it needs more care than it does after it has weathered a few storms. When you are in this young and tender stage of your growth, be an observer of those who are exhibiting the fruit of the Holy Spirit in their lives. If the fruit is good, the tree is probably good. Pick up what you can from other believers in Christ. However, when reading your Bible, be sure the conclusions you reach by your observations are indeed supported by Scriptures.

## Principle #3 — Fellowship creates righteous boundaries.

One of the first principles God taught me as a pastor was that people in trouble tend to withdraw from fellowship. When things are going well in our relationship with God and our Christian family, being around others is easy and uplifting. There is a genuine joy in the exchanges of life. When something is wrong, however, the unresolved issues of our spirit man make us uncomfortable being around others who are walking in spiritual wholeness.

In order to remain in fellowship (or hang out with the group), we will eventually have to deal with the areas that are in need of attention. Let me overstate the principle for emphasis. You might find it difficult to get drunk and then go to a prayer meeting. While that may seem obvious, the same is true of jealously, envy, strife, sexual impurity or any number of other habits or attitudes that can pollute the inner man. If this internal pollution is not addressed, it will eventually separate us from the group and the God that gives us life. The thought of losing life-giving fellowship can be a strong motivator to resolve issues and deal with sins.

"And let us consider one another to provoke unto love and to good works:

Not forsaking the assembling of ourselves together, as the manner of some is; but exhorting one another: and so much the more, as ye see the day approaching."                              **Hebrews 10:24,25**

## Principle #4 — Fellowship brings fulfillment.

As time passes and your growth continues, your fellowship with the family of Christian believers will begin to take on different roles. It won't take you long to realize that God birthed a family full of different gifts and callings. No matter how much you grow and how serious you are, you will never be able to say to the rest of the church that you don't need them. God has wisely designed a family that needs each other's gifts in order to succeed. The bad news is that you cannot ultimately succeed without the support and talents of others. The good news is that they cannot ultimately succeed without your support and talents.

This series of teachings is not the result of one person's determination and talent. While one person wrote, another edited. Another designed the web site, while another laid out the book. Someone else worked on the graphics, while others creatively got the word out. Mentors are helping new believers, while givers support the staff and costs of the ministry. Printers print, shippers ship, secretaries answer the phone and administrators coordinate the flow of information that makes everything continue to work. How can any of the necessary pieces in this spiritual puzzle say to the others, "I don't need you"?

The sooner you realize that you are only one small part of what God is doing, the sooner you will become grateful that you are allowed to serve in the place God has gifted you. This humble gratitude is healthy and will allow you to serve without an attitude. You will learn that God doesn't have any "special" children. He does have children with different gifts, but whatever our gifts are, we will always need each other.

It is indeed liberating to come to that inevitable conclusion. I need you to be what God called you to be, and you need me to be what God called me to be. As we learn to honor and prefer one another, strife and pride disappear. The picture of a church grateful for its gifts and serving others with humility is one that the world needs to see. When you find that place, you will also find true fulfillment in your Christian life.

The right kind of fellowship is so important. We want you to help us help you find a Christian family (church) near you. When you finish these lessons, please fill out the follow-up form and E-mail it to our web site. We will forward your information to a balanced, Bible-believing church in your area that will welcome you into the family of believers. They stand ready to pick up where these lessons finish. Please don't neglect to make this necessary next step in your Christian growth.

*Discussion Points:*

1. Why should you limit fellowship with your old life?

2. Why do unresolved issues and sin keep you from fellowship with your new Christian friends?

3. How can Christian fellowship keep you from sin?

4. How does fellowship lead to fulfillment?

*Memory Verse:*

**For the body is not one member, but many.**
**1 Corinthians 12:14**

## Lesson #13
# The Holy Spirit

When Jesus' earthly ministry was nearing an end and He knew He was going to return to Heaven, He shared some very important information with His disciples. He had been with them from the beginning of their faith and was the stabilizing force for all those who believed. When questions arose or persecutions increased, when the sick needed healing or the devil needed rebuking, Jesus was always there to take the initiative to address the issue at hand. The disciples could always retreat into the protective shadow of their teacher. He was the perpetual answer to their endless questions. But all of that was about to change in a big way.

Jesus was fully aware of the role He was playing in the disciples' lives and knew that His return to Heaven would leave a huge void. In preparation for His departure He told them that, after He left, a replacement would come to pick up where He had left off. This crucial job of being an advisor, helper and teacher to the disciples was given to God the Holy Spirit. The Holy Spirit is indeed God and is referred to as God throughout the Scriptures. Who else but a member of the Godhead could step into Jesus' shoes and be what Jesus was to the Church?

"And I will pray the Father, and He shall give you another Comforter, that He may abide with you for ever;

> Even the Spirit of truth; whom the world cannot receive, because it seeth Him not, neither knoweth Him: but ye know Him; for He dwelleth with you, and shall be in you."
>
> **John 14:16,17**

It is interesting that Jesus told them that this Comforter had already been with them but now was going to be in them. The Holy Spirit was in Jesus, and it was by the empowering of the Holy Spirit that He fulfilled His earthly ministry. When Jesus said that the Holy Spirit had been with them, He spoke the truth. Now this same Spirit that had been in Jesus from the beginning of His ministry was going to be sent to indwell and fill them. The power of Jesus' ministry would now empower them to continue the work of the Kingdom of God here on earth.

> "And Jesus being full of the Holy Ghost returned from Jordan, and was led by the Spirit into the wilderness."
>
> **Luke 4:1**

Jesus knew that, without this indwelling and empowering of the Holy Spirit, the disciples would never be able to fulfill their destiny. He instructed them to return to Jerusalem and not leave until they were endued with this power from on high.

*Luke 24:49* says it this way:

> "And, behold, I send the promise of My Father upon you: but tarry ye in the city of Jerusalem, until ye be endued with power from on high."

That promise was fulfilled a few days later when the disciples were in an upper room in Jerusalem and the Holy Spirit came to live in the disciples. The stated primary purpose of this relationship between the disciples and the Holy Spirit was to aid them in their assignment to be witnesses to mankind. It is the heritage of all who believe on Jesus Christ as their Savior to be filled with the Holy Spirit and enjoy all the benefits of that relationship. If Jesus relied on the Holy Spirit to be His partner in ministry, how grateful we should be that this same relationship is available to us.

The Holy Spirit brings a lot to this partnership. The Holy Spirit, as God with us, brings God's power and character to live inside us. The power of God is expressed through the gifts of the Spirit, and God's character through the fruit of the Spirit. It is important to remember that gifts are *given*; therefore, the fact that someone has a gift doesn't mean the person is mature in his faith. Fruit, on the other hand, is *grown* and is a result of a relationship with the tree. We should spend some time growing fruit before we try to show off our gifts!

### The Fruit of the Spirit

**"But the fruit of the Spirit is** *love, joy, peace, long-suffering, gentleness, goodness, faith,*

*Meekness, temperance:* **against such there is no law."**

**Galatians 5:22,23**

As you spend time exploring your relationship with God, you will find that He *is* love, joy, peace and the other characteristics listed above. Because He now lives in you, you will also find that your nature and motivations will begin to draw from God's character. When you are unable or incapable of right responses to situations, your internal life partner (the Holy Spirit) will help you choose a response that is pleasing to God. Pray that your life bathes others in the same divine love and character that has touched yours.

### The Gifts of the Spirit

**"But the manifestation of the Spirit is given to every man to profit withal.**

> **For to one is given by the Spirit the *word of wisdom*; to another the *word of knowledge* by the same Spirit;**
>
> **To another *faith* by the same Spirit; to another the *gifts of healing* by the same Spirit;**
>
> **To another the *working of miracles*; to another *prophecy*; to another *discerning of spirits*; to another *divers kinds of tongues*; to another the *interpretation of tongues*:**
>
> **But all these worketh that one and the selfsame Spirit, dividing to every man severally as he will."**
>
> **1 Corinthians 12:7-11**

These gifts from God enable us to go beyond human talents or training. They are a direct result of a relationship with God through which He gives us abilities that are beyond the natural way of doing things. For instance, doctors may be trained in the science of medicine, but the gift of healing can operate through those to whom it is given even though they have no medical training. Believers may pray in a heavenly language that they have never studied. God's way gives someone the ability to give wise counsel even though they may not be educated. The purpose of these gifts is to serve others who are in need and to be witnesses of God's love to mankind.

As was said earlier, if you have been given a gift, it is yours. If God gave it to you, it will work. The fact that you have a gift, however, doesn't mean you are mature. It is important to remember the reason God gives gifts. They are given to bless others and witness for Him. You will find if you seek gifts, you are more likely to have problems than if you first seek character. If the desire of your heart is to have Jesus' character, the gifts will come.

Whatever you do, live your life seeking to please God and to bless others, and you will find fulfillment.

> "Even so ye, forasmuch as ye are zealous of spiritual gifts, seek that ye may excel to the edifying of the church."
>
> 1 Corinthians 14:12

As you live your life and begin to recognize more and more that still small voice of the Holy Spirit inside your heart, you will find that He too is God. The same love, gratitude and respect you feel for God the Father and Jesus the Son, you will begin to express to God the Holy Spirit. He too is worthy of our love. The further He leads you on the road of truth and righteousness, the more you will appreciate His ministry in your life.

> "In whom ye also trusted, after that ye heard the word of truth, the gospel of your salvation: in whom also after that ye believed, ye were sealed with that holy Spirit of promise,
>
> Which is the earnest of our inheritance (down payment) until the redemption of the purchased possession, unto the praise of his glory."
>
> Ephesians 1:13,14

Another of the Holy Spirit's roles in your life is to lead you to the truth. Jesus said that when the Holy Spirit was in the life of a believer, He would teach him all things. Since God cannot lie or contradict Himself, the leadership of the Spirit will always be in complete agreement with the Scriptures. As you read your Bible, ask the Holy Spirit to help you understand what you are reading. You will be amazed at what you will begin to understand.

*Discussion Points:*

1. How did the Holy Spirit replace the ministry of Jesus in the life of the believer?

2. What is the purpose of the fruit of the Spirit in the believer?

3. What is the purpose of the gifts of the Spirit in the believer?

4. How does the Holy Spirit lead us into truth?

*Memory Verse:*

**And I will pray the Father, and he shall give you another Comforter, that he may abide with you for ever.**

**John 14:16**

# Lesson #14
# Laying on of Hands

At a first look it wouldn't seem that the laying on of hands would be included as one of the foundational doctrines of the Church. It is included, however, in the list in Hebrews 6, as an essential principle needed for building a balanced faith. Remember that the Christian faith is one that deals with a supernatural world interacting with the natural world. Aside from man's measurable, physical existence, another part of mankind exists. The custom or doctrine of laying on of hands is one avenue by which the reality of the spiritual world at times finds its way into people's lives.

## Principle #1 — The laying on of hands was used to impart blessing.

In the Old Testament the right hand was considered the hand of blessing, and the left hand was considered lesser or unclean. When a father was about to die, he would call his sons before him to bless them. He would lay his right hand on the oldest son to pass on the family blessing and his left hand on the others. A blessing could also be passed from grandfather to grandson. Such was the case when Jacob (Israel) was about to die and Joseph took his two sons to see their grandfather. When Joseph presented them to receive Israel's blessing, he positioned the first born Manasseh in front of Israel's right hand and the younger Ephraim toward his left hand. Yet when Israel stretched out his hands to bless the boys, he crossed his arms, putting his right hand on Ephraim and his left hand on Manasseh.

This occurrence troubled Joseph, for he was expecting the family blessing to go to the older, Manasseh. When Joseph asked his father what he was doing, Israel's response was simple — that the blessing was going to be passed on to the younger Ephraim. Israel knew what he was doing. He had intended to bless the younger. The amazing factor was that God accepted Israel's prayer, and thus the blessing of the firstborn followed Ephraim throughout his life. How could something as simple as placing one hand or another on the head of someone make a difference in the outcome of that person's life?

> "And Joseph took them both, Ephraim in his right hand toward Israel's left hand, and Manasseh in his left hand toward Israel's right hand, and brought them near unto him.
>
> And Israel stretched out his right hand, and laid it upon Ephraim's head, who was the younger, and his left hand upon Manasseh's head, guiding his hands wittingly; for Manasseh was the firstborn.
>
> And he blessed Joseph, and said, God, before whom my fathers Abraham and Isaac did walk, the God which fed me all my life long unto this day,
>
> The Angel which redeemed me from all evil, bless the lads; and let my name be named on them, and the name of my fathers Abraham and Isaac; and let them grow into a multitude in the midst of the earth.
>
> And when Joseph saw that his father laid his right hand upon the head of Ephraim, it displeased him: and he held up his father's hand, to remove it from Ephraim's head unto Manasseh's head.

> And Joseph said unto his father, Not so, my father: for this is the firstborn; put thy right hand upon his head."
>
> Genesis 48:13-20

> "And his father refused, and said, I know it, my son, I know it: he also shall become a people, and he also shall be great: but truly his younger brother shall be greater than he, and his seed shall become a multitude of nations.
>
> And he blessed them that day, saying, In thee shall Israel bless, saying, God make thee as Ephraim and as Manasseh: and he set Ephraim before Manasseh."
>
> Genesis 48:19,20

On a spiritual level, God partners with His people, and imparts, confirms and accepts by reaching through them to others. It is as if, at times, His people are literally His own hands extended. When hands are laid on others in accordance with God's will, there is a transfer of power which is as real as handing someone a gift. The laying on of hands was such a part of the Jewish culture that, when Jesus was ministering, the people brought Him their children so that He would lay His hands on them and pray a blessing upon them. Even in our natural society we rub children on the head to let them know we love them.

> "Then were there brought unto him little children, that He should put His hands on them, and pray."
>
> Matthew 19:13

## Principle #2 — The laying on of hands was used to impart healing.

The laying on of hands also plays an important role in imparting healing. Jesus would often lay hands on the sick, and they would recover. Scripture presents an interesting account of a woman who received healing from Jesus, but in a strange reversal that gives insight as to how the power to heal works. Jesus and the disciples were passing through a crowd. All at once, Jesus stopped and asked His disciples who had touched Him.

> "And Jesus said, Somebody hath touched Me: for I perceive that virtue is gone out of Me."
>
> **Luke 8:46**

The disciples were confused because so many people were around, anyone could have touched Him. Jesus stopped, however, not because someone had bumped into Him, but because someone had touched Him by faith and had literally pulled healing power out of Him. The word *virtue* in the above passage could just as easily be translated "power." The faith of the woman had pulled healing power from Jesus, and He had felt it leave His body. God's power is so real that, when it moves from one person to another, sometimes the exchange can be felt. This very real giving of a gift of healing is more often transferred from the one who has the gift to the one who needs it, by the laying on of hands.

> "And besought him greatly, saying, My little daughter lieth at the point of death: I pray thee, come and lay Thy hands on her, that she may be healed; and she shall live."
>
> **Mark 5:23**

> "Now when the sun was setting, all they that had any sick with divers diseases brought them unto Him; and He laid His hands on every one of them, and healed them."
>
> **Luke 4:40**

As believers in Jesus, we can partner with God in imparting His divine power to make a difference in the lives of hurting people. Jesus laid His hands on the sick and His touch made a difference in their condition. So we too can lay hands on those who are ill and expect changed conditions. That same power which operated through Jesus can operate through us when it is needed.

> "...they shall lay hands on the sick, and they shall recover."
>
> Mark 16:18b

## Principle #3 — The laying on of hands was used to set people apart for service.

Other blessings and gifts are sometimes imparted through the laying on of hands. When it was time for Paul and Barnabas to be sent out from the church at Antioch, there was a time of prayer and fasting. Just before they were sent out, the leadership of the church laid hands on them. The message being delivered was simple: We are with you, and we believe in you; go with God's blessing.

> "And when they had fasted and prayed, and laid their hands on them, they sent them away."
>
> Acts 13:3

When praying for others, it is entirely appropriate to lay hands on them, usually on the head or shoulders, (keep it pure) to impart what gifts you may have. Even beyond that, you have the unique opportunity to show sympathy, support, approval, compassion or encouragement by the simple act of touching someone in need.

*Discussion Points:*

1. How were hands used in Israel to impart blessings?

2. How is healing imparted through the laying on of hands?

3. What is the importance of laying on of hands in confirming spiritual gifts?

4. How did Jesus know there was something different when the woman touched Him?

*Memory Verse:*

**...they shall lay hands on the sick, and they shall recover.**

**Mark 16:18b**

## Lesson #15

# Forgiveness

The words of the Lord's prayer are powerful in their potential when they say, "Forgive us as we forgive those who trespass against us." The first part of the passage points to man's need for Heaven's forgiveness. We as a people are in desperate need to be reconciled to God. The sad truth is that there is little that can be done from our side to set things right. Nothing that man has or anything he could do could address the fact that man's sin created a breach in his relationship with God. The good news is that our problem was important enough to God that He set a plan in motion to adequately address the need.

### Principle #1 — Man needs forgiveness.

The truth is that man found himself separated from God by his rebellion and sin. The same pride that separated Adam and Eve from God's plan would eventually visit each of us with its same devastating effect. Once that separation occurred, we were left without a remedy for the offense. You see, life has taught us that when there is an offense, somebody has to pay. The problem is that none of the resources available to mankind was sufficient to satisfy the price required to set things right.

## Principle #2 — God provided the price for our forgiveness.

Thanks be to God that He had pity on us in our need and provided the price necessary to cancel the debt we owed for our sins. When Jesus came to earth in human form, He came with a purpose. He came to give Himself as the payment in full for all our transgressions. The offering of His own life for ours was declared payment in full for all our offenses. This supreme gift opened for all who will believe an entrance into Heaven.

For this Heaven-inspired plan to work, there was one vital truth that was required. God had to be willing to forgive. If God had decided there was no way He could ever put aside our offenses and be willing to have a relationship with us again, we would have been locked forever in hopeless separation. We should be grateful that such wasn't the case. God, who is rich in mercy, loved us enough to set aside His right to be mad and hurt by our actions, and to forgive us.

> "If we confess our sins, He is faithful and just to forgive our sins and to cleanse us of all unrighteousness."
> 
> 1 John 1:9

Without question, the most powerful gift God ever gave us was His forgiveness. When God forgives, He separates our offenses from us as far as the east is from the west. He doesn't keep old records of our offenses. He doesn't continually remind us of our past failures. This ability of God to grant us a new beginning and relate to us as if we had never sinned is a remarkable quality indeed. In fact, the concept is so foreign to our old nature that it is difficult at times to believe. We pray for forgiveness and then struggle with the fact that God says, "Yes, I will forgive."

*Forgiveness*

Because of our belief that somebody has to pay, if we are not careful, we can miss out on the greatest of all offers. The truth is that somebody has already paid. The challenge presented to us is one of deciding whether or not we will accept the fact that the price Jesus paid at Calvary for our sins was received by God as payment in full. Failure to understand fully God's offer could leave us in the unhealthy position of trying to punish ourselves. People do crazy things when they don't feel forgiven. I think most of the self-destructive behavior people find themselves in is due to the fact that they have never found or accepted true forgiveness.

As a young Christian, I struggled with the fact that God was really willing to forgive me. Satan would taunt me with the accusation that God hadn't forgiven me. As I was praying one day, God asked me the following question in my mind: "Where are your sins?" My answer seemed too simple. I responded that the blood of Jesus covered them. Then God gave me a powerful bit of understanding. He replied, "Then tell the devil, if he will go to the blood of Jesus and take your sins out and bring them to you, that you will accept responsibility for your past sins. If however, he cannot present your forgiven sins to you, then he should go away and never mention those sins again." That was thirty years ago, and I haven't heard anymore about it. The devil has no power or right to torment you with sins that have been confessed and forsaken.

Once you finally do believe that God really meant what He said and you accept His offer to forgive your sins, the most wonderful thing happens. The heaviness of your guilt lifts and is replaced with a joy and peace that can be found no place else. When the sentence of death is removed, the joy of a clean heart is like nothing else in this life. This wondrous retreat will be available throughout your life. Jesus' payment for your sins was not just for the offenses committed before you were born again. Forgiveness from God is available throughout your life whenever it is accompanied with real repentance (Lesson #17).

The opening statement of forgiveness in the Lord's prayer has a curious opportunity. It clearly says that forgiveness will be extended to us in the same way and to the same degree as we are willing to forgive others. It is possible to enhance or deepen our own experience of forgiveness by the way we treat others who are in need of our forgiveness.

Are we truly willing to give up our right to be hurt and to extend the healing hand of forgiveness to others who have hurt us? Remember that God is able to give us the gift of forgiveness because He was the offended party. So often we harbor our hurt simply because we feel we have that right because we were the one offended. We retreat to the "but you don't know what they did to me" argument. Forgiveness is a willful giving up of our right to be hurt for the sake of the well being and wholeness of the person who wronged us. Forgiving is not easy to do. Hurts are not easy to release. Yet, to the same degree we are willing to release others of the debt they owe us, God is willing to release us of the debt we owe Him. Powerful, isn't it?

## Principle #3 — The Father's heart forgives.

There is a remarkable example of this truth in the Scriptures. In *Luke 15* in the story of the prodigal son, we find a selfish son who takes his inheritance and wastes it on a lifestyle that leads him to financial and spiritual poverty. How his father's heart must have broken when he saw all his dreams and hopes for his son walk out the door of selfishness. That father had every right to harden his heart to protect it from further hurt. The miracle and example of God's forgiveness, however, is the higher path which the father took.

When his son returned home sometime later, the father didn't make him grovel and shed tears. The father's response was Godlike in that he welcomed his son home without conditions or repayment of the squandered inheritance. Instead, the father threw a party and restored his son to his place in the family. That father's forgiveness that kept no record of offenses is the kind of love that relieves people of their heavy burden of guilt.

## Principle #4 — We are most like God when we forgive.

Let me ask you a question. When are we most like God? When we see the opportunity to relieve people of their heavy burdens and lay aside our own hurts to see others restored, we are partners with God in the greatest ministry of all. Jesus said that He came to undo the heavy burdens and let the oppressed go free. When we love others more than ourselves, so as to undo their heavy burdens by forgiveness, we are most like God.

So, how do you find the power to release people of the emotional debts you feel they owe you for the hurts they may have caused? When Jesus was on the cross, He prayed to his father, "Forgive them for they know not what they do." Ask yourself this question: "If the people who hurt me love God with all their hearts and want to please Him, would they have intentionally hurt someone for whom Jesus died?" We must admit that, if a person truly loves God and has had a heart change, he will want the best for us, just as we want the best for others.

The problem is that, with all the hurts in the world, humanity has not yet learned to love with God's love. What Jesus was trying to tell us when He was on the cross was that, if the people who were crucifying Him had really known what they were doing, they wouldn't have done it.

All God asks of us is to carry His heart of forgiveness on earth just as Jesus did. As we become more like God, we find ourselves wanting for this world what God wants for the world. We begin to understand the partnership with Heaven, referred to in the following passage from the Lord's prayer: "Father let Your Kingdom come on earth as it is in Heaven." We should do everything in our power to help people find forgiveness. Sometimes they must be touched by our forgiveness before they can even hope to believe God would ever forgive them.

After we have walked the Christian life for some time, we won't need forgiveness anymore, right? Wrong. The Christian life is a lifelong journey that leads us from one discovery to another as we grow in our knowledge of God's will. As new areas of our lives are exposed to the wisdom of Godly living, the only thing that makes sense is to forsake the old way of living and change to accept the truths we find as we grow. When we see the foolishness of the way we were previously living, we often find ourselves in need of God's forgiveness. Aren't you glad that He always forgives?

Wouldn't it be wonderful if we had the reputation of always being forgiving with everyone? We wouldn't hold grudges or have points to prove; we would simply want others to find the same peace we have found in our relationship with God. When such forgiveness is the motivation of our lives, we will never have to worry whether God will accept us or forgive our next offense. He will always be there like the father of the prodigal son. God loves us so much that, once we come to our senses like the son in the story, He is simply glad to see us and restore fellowship.

Don't let your pride or hurt keep you from the sheer joy of bathing in the sweet waters of God's forgiveness. Once you find your own peace with God, look for ways to lift the heavy burdens of others. Giving what you have received completes the cycle of life.

*Discussion Points:*
1. Why does man need forgiveness?
2. How was the price paid for your forgiveness?
3. Describe the Father's heart of forgiveness.
4. When are we most like God?

*Memory Verse:*

**Be ye kind one to another tenderhearted forgiving one another even as God for Christ's sake hath forgiven you.**

**Ephesians 4:32**

## Lesson #16
# Fasting

Fasting is admittedly not the most exciting doctrine of the Church. The thought of doing without anything is not appealing, much less doing without food. In order to participate in this or any other part of the Christian life, it is important to understand why God included certain doctrines as part of our Christian culture. Before you skip this teaching and go on to something more appealing, please take the time to find out why God included it and how He wants to bless you by fasting.

### Principle #1 — Fasting is a statement of priorities.

From time to time life may present you with challenges which are simply too much for you to deal with. When a loved one is sick or you find yourself at a crossroads in your life, where do you turn? Throughout the Scriptures, when dire circumstances arose for God's people, there were times when hearing from God became a higher priority than eating. Such is the essence of fasting. While fasting usually includes doing without food, there is much more to this Christian experience.

Let me share with you an example from the book of Esther. The Jewish people were in captivity in Persia and in danger of being destroyed. Command had already been given that they were to be killed. Esther had become the queen of the country, but nobody in the king's court knew she was a Jew except her cousin Mordecai. The only way to stop the slaughter appeared to be for Esther to intercede directly to the king for her people's lives. To do so would mean she would have to reveal the fact that she too was a Jew.

As you might imagine, this was not an easy thing for Esther to do. She would have to go before the king unannounced. In that country, if she intruded into the king's court without being invited, she could be put to death on the spot unless he acknowledged her by extending to her the royal scepter. For her to take such a risk, she wanted to have every advantage before she went in before the king. When messengers from Mordecai came to see if she would indeed intercede to the king for her people, she responded as follows:

**"Then Esther bade them return Mordecai this answer,**

**Go, gather together all the Jews that are present in Shushan, and fast ye for me, and neither eat nor drink three days, night or day: I also and my maidens will fast likewise; and so will I go in unto the king, which is not according to the law: and if I perish, I perish."**

**Esther 4:15,16**

When life presents you with one of those moments in which the future looks totally disastrous and you see no hope, you too may find that food and water are less important to you than knowing God is with you. Oh, it is important to note that the king accepted Esther, and the Jewish people were miraculously spared. God's favor is worth everything.

## Principle #2 — Fasting is a private experience between you and God.

It is also important to know that Jesus taught the principle of fasting in the Sermon on the Mount. From what He had to say, it didn't appear that fasting is only for some of us. The Word clearly states *when* you fast, not, *if* you fast. Fasting is never to be done to impress others. Clean yourself up and go about your business as usual. After all, it is God's favor you are seeking, not your neighbor's.

**"Moreover when ye fast, be not, as the hypocrites, of a sad countenance: for they disfigure their faces, that they may appear unto men to fast. Verily I say unto you, They have their reward.**

**But thou, when thou fastest, anoint thine head, and wash thy face;**

**That thou appear not unto men to fast, but unto thy Father which is in secret: and Thy Father, which seeth in secret, shall reward thee openly."**

**Matthew 6:16-18**

## Principle #3 — Do not fast too long.

When you first begin to explore the practice of fasting, you should note some interesting points. Fasting does not guarantee that the issue which led you to fast in the first place will work out to your benefit. The purpose of the fast is to diminish your physical appetites and thereby bring an increased sensitivity to the part of you that hears God's voice. Once you hear from God, you are more likely to hear something about your spiritual growth than you are to hear a big heavenly "YES" to your problem.

After the first day or two of fasting, your body takes second place to your spirit; the sense of closeness to God is unmistakable. Your hunger disappears and your body seems to be running on air. There is a sense of communion with God that is very satisfying. You can't live this way forever, of course, but the response of your spirit is so fulfilling that you may find yourself having a difficult time knowing when to end the fast.

Before you begin to fast, study the Scriptures to broaden your knowledge about the subject. Ask God to help you determine the guidelines of the fast. Determine the maximum length you might fast.

Once you have begun the fast, if you go without food more than three days, pay close attention to your body. Usually when you get hungry after three days, your fast is over. Spiritual points are not awarded for how long you fast, but rather for how well you hear. I have had friends who couldn't quit a fast because they felt guilty. Avoiding guilt is never a good reason for continuing a fast.

If you are going to fast more than two or three days, you should drink lots of water. When Jesus fasted in the wilderness for forty days, the Bible says that, after He was finished, He was hungry. It doesn't say He was thirsty. Your kidneys will begin to shut down after a few days if you don't drink water. You can survive without food for forty days, but not without water.

> "Being forty days tempted of the devil. And in those days he did eat nothing: and when they were ended, he afterward hungered."
> 
> Luke 4:2

## Principle #4 — God's Chosen Fast

> "Is not this the fast that I have chosen? to loose the bands of wickedness, to undo the heavy burdens, and to let the oppressed go free, and that ye break every yoke?

*Fasting*

Is it not to deal thy bread to the hungry, and that thou bring the poor that are cast out to thy house? when thou seest the naked, that thou cover him; and that thou hide not thyself from thine own flesh?"

Isaiah 58:6,7

Of all the different ways and forms of fasting denoted in the Scriptures, the highest form is one that calls us to a different way of living. Leading a fasted life means denying our own needs for the sake of others. When we live to lift the burdens of others, feed the hungry, clothe the naked and care for the needs of our family, we are living a life that says to others, "God cares for you." People are struggling to find evidence that God loves them. When we are willing to put our own needs aside in order to help others, and we act with a pure heart, God assures us that He will respond with a blessing. Read the promises in this passage of Scripture; they are amazing.

"Then shall thy light break forth as the morning, and thine health shall spring forth speedily: and thy righteousness shall go before thee; the glory of the LORD shall be Thy rereward (protection).

Then shalt thou call, and the LORD shall answer; thou shalt cry, and He shall say, Here I am. If thou take away from the midst of thee the yoke, the putting forth of the finger, and speaking vanity;

And if thou draw out thy soul to the hungry, and satisfy the afflicted soul; then shall thy light rise in obscurity, and thy darkness be as the noonday:

And the LORD shall guide thee continually, and satisfy thy soul in drought, and make fat thy bones: and thou shalt be like a watered garden, and like a spring of water, whose waters fail not.

And they that shall be of thee shall build the old waste places: thou shalt raise up the foundations of many generations; and thou shalt be called, The repairer of the breach, The restorer of paths to dwell in."

**Isaiah 58:8-12**

Who wouldn't want all these benefits in life? As you grow in your relationship with God, you will find Him reaching through you to bless others. Avoid the temptation to rush the process. God is balanced and patient. Remember that, with God, obedience is better than sacrifice (1 Samuel 15:22). If you do it His way, you get His blessing in your life.

*Discussion Points:*

1. How is fasting a statement of priorities?
2. Should you tell all your friends that you are fasting?
3. How do you know when to stop a fast?
4. What is God's chosen fast?

*Memory Verse:*

**Is not this the fast that I have chosen? to loose the bands of wickedness, to undo the heavy burdens, and to let the oppressed go free, and that ye break every yoke?**

**Isaiah 58:6**

## Lesson #17
# Repentance

I am sure that at some time during your life you have seen someone standing on a sidewalk or in the stands at an athletic event holding a sign with big letters spelling out REPENT. This clear, one-word message strikes at the essence of man's common need. The sad truth is, however, that man has grossly misunderstood God's intentions in the doctrine of repentance.

For many the term *repent* smacks of a confrontational accusation of man's shortcomings. The feeling in the air surrounding the word *repentance* is that man has messed up so badly, God is about to lose it and squash him like a bug. The feeling is, "You better hurry up, cry, and act sorry, or you are going to pay. Oh yeah, and if you don't shed tears, you aren't really serious and haven't really repented."

### Principle #1 — Sorrow alone is not enough.

While true repentance may include tears, they are not required. The confusion on this subject is due partially to the fact that the word *repentance* is used in several different ways in the Scriptures. In this discussion we will only cover the two primary uses. The first use of repentance refers to the response of someone who is caught committing a wrong and is sorry because he is about to be punished. This kind of repentance is referred to in *Matthew 27:3* when Judas repented after he betrayed Jesus. We know from other Scriptures that Judas wasn't saved; consequently, his repentance was not the kind that leads to a restored relationship with God. Just feeling bad because you did something bad does not mean that you have repented.

The bad feeling we get when we hurt someone is our conscience speaking to us. Conscience is the inner voice of God we are all born with that continually urges us to do the right thing. When we violate this inner voice, we know immediately all is not well. Something inside us tells us we shouldn't expect to be blessed for our disobedience. In fact, we are not surprised when all is not well. Even though we may complain that we shouldn't have to experience this bad feeling or the consequences of our actions, we know inwardly that we are at odds with God's will. How do we know? Because we made decisions contrary to His inner urgings.

At this point, we have a decision to make. Do we simply go on with life, waiting for the ax to fall, or do we take some proactive steps to restore the broken fellowship? If we decide to wait and wait and do nothing, life will be twisted up inside us, as we try to ignore the fact that things aren't right. Quite possibly, we will feel terrible about the situation. We must remember, though, that feeling bad is not the same as repenting.

The kind of repentance God is looking for is the kind that causes us to change the way we live and not just try to avoid the consequences of our actions. After all, would we as parents rather hear our children yell that they are sorry as we discipline them, or have them come to us and apologize before we find out there is a problem? God is more interested in His children's long-term commitment to His principles than He is in making them pay for their last mistake.

## Principle #2 — Repentance is not a demand but an invitation.

Once we really believe God is on our side and wants the best for us, the awkwardness of coming to Him with our problems goes away. What exactly is Biblical repentance? And why does God want us to repent? The best description of Biblical repentance is that it is a change in the direction we are going, a change in how we think about our way of life. If we are going in a wrong direction, away from God and His principles, we are invited by the Holy Spirit to turn around and pursue God rather than avoid Him.

We humans have a common problem. We believe we can take care of ourselves. Often, we find ourselves running after things that won't bring lasting fulfillment or satisfaction. Eventually, the emptiness of self-directed living leaves us aimless. When God sees us in such a state, He issues the invitation to change directions and return to our relationship with Him. When we accept this divine invitation and change the direction of our lives, turning back to God, we have repented. Sometimes this decision is accompanied with tears and other times with sober resolve. Whatever the emotion, the change of direction is the important thing.

Now it is easy to see why Jesus came preaching repentance. Only when we turn to God and involve Him in our daily lives and decisions can we ever hope to make sense out of life. In the book of Revelation one of the churches was encouraged to *be zealous and repent*. This phrase literally means to "run eagerly to the opportunity to restore your dialogue with Heaven." Only when life is connected to the Creator can we ever find true fulfillment.

## Principle #3 — Real repentance means a change in the direction of your life.

To take full advantage of God's offer is to see it through until there is a lasting change in lifestyle. The initial change of direction is the first step that should lead to a permanent, new way of living. God is not just trying to patch you up after your last failure, but is offering a partnership that will lead you away from the destructive place you used to live. Seeking absolution for the past (Lesson #15 — Forgiveness), as well as seeking direction for the future, is the fuller picture of the process of repentance. The end of the experience is intended to leave you in a better place, with a new lifestyle.

Let me give you a simple example. If you were stealing from your employer, the Holy Spirit would tell you (inwardly) to stop and make restitution. If somehow, you justified your actions and continued ignoring the inner voice, in time, you would find yourself empty inside because you were out of fellowship with God. This lack of fulfillment would lead you to the conclusion that something was desperately wrong. Your soul-searching would cause you to determine that you need God in your life. You would purpose to seek God and would hold His Word internally as the standard by which to live. During this process you would decide that stealing is not acceptable behavior. You would return what was wrongfully taken, resolving never again to revert to such a lifestyle.

Why was God so upset with Capernaum in *Matthew 11:21-24*? Scripture tells us, if the mighty works Capernaum saw Jesus perform had been seen by those

*Repentance*

in Sodom, all Sodom would have repented. In other words, although the city of Capernaum saw the miracles of Jesus and rejoiced, when the miracles were all over, the people didn't change the way they lived. The reason Jesus performed the miracles in the first place was to encourage Capernaum to forsake their empty, self-willed lifestyles and adopt righteous ways of living. Yet after they basked in the glory of Jesus' life and ministry, they went right back to their old ways of lying, cheating and living for themselves.

When you adjust your lifestyle out of respect for God's place in your life, you are on the path to true repentance. Certainly, you will experience Godly sorrow, sorrow which may be expressed in a number of ways and may or may not include outward emotions. Remember, *Hebrews 6:1* says you are to repent from dead works. You are to stop living the kind of life filled with things which have no eternal perspective and begin living an eternally significant life. Whatever the expression, if you are left with hope for a future with God, and you have peace about the past, based upon God's Word, you have probably experienced true repentance.

It is impossible to live in this world and do everything right all the time. This much I do know, however, when you live your life out of a genuine desire to find the will of God and do it, you will find meaning and fulfillment. If along the way you find yourself off the straight and narrow, be zealous and repent. God is waiting for you to turn around and restore fellowship with Him.

*Discussion Points:*

1. Is just being sorry for a wrong enough to make things right with God?

2. Why does God want you to repent?

3. What are dead works?
4. Define true repentance.

*Memory Verse:*

**Repent ye therefore, and be converted, that your sins may be blotted out, when the times of refreshing shall come from the presence of the Lord.**

**Acts 3:19**

## Lesson #18
# New Jerusalem

Admittedly, as wonderful as the Christian life is, it still isn't easy. The devil hates you. The world doesn't want you to succeed. Some people close to you don't appreciate how important your relationship with God is to you. Worst of all, sometimes you seem to lose your focus and behave in ways contrary to your Christian convictions. Just how do you keep yourself on track for a lifetime? Where do you find the motivation to continue to say no to the world's attempts to pull you away from the pureness of the Christian life?

> **"Keep yourself unspotted from the world."**
> **James 1:27b**

I believe one of the reasons Christians lose their way in life is that they do not have a clear internal picture of eternity. If you as a Christian are unable to visualize the reward you may find at the end of a venture, it will be difficult to pay the price. The fact is, what God has prepared for you in eternity is beyond anything you can ask or think.

> **"But as it is written, Eye hath not seen, nor ear heard, neither have entered into the heart of man, the things which God hath prepared for them that love him."**
> **1 Corinthians 2:9**

While we in this life never will comprehend fully all the wonders of the life to come, the Scriptures do give us some brief glimpses of what we can expect. From the very beginning of God's relationship with man, there has been the promise of an eternal dwelling place. There is an eternal reward waiting for those who qualify. While most Christians believe this will be a beautiful place where God lives, few can offer a description with any details. It certainly will be better than a rocking chair on the front porch of a cabin in Heaven; I can assure you.

> **"For he looked for a city which hath foundations, whose builder and maker is God."**
>
> **Hebrews 11:10**

The city Abraham was looking for in Genesis is described in *Revelation 21* as the New Jerusalem. Built by God, the city comes down from the heavens to rest on earth where it serves as the eternal home of God and His saints. If you were God and had all the resources of eternity available to you, what kind of place would you build for your eternal home? Remember that we have been invited to live there with Him, so this is going to be a huge place.

Scripture tells us that the city is 1500 miles long, 1500 miles wide and 1500 miles high. To give you an idea of how big that is, imagine a city from Chicago to Mexico and from Denver to Atlanta, all under one roof. The surface area covered by the city is 2,250,000 square miles. It is so high that an airplane cannot fly around it; a space shuttle is needed. The outer surface of the city is covered in pure gold. If this heavenly siding were only $1/8$ th of an inch thick, at today's price of gold, the value of the covering would be over 56 quadrillion US dollars.

The foundation is made from a variety of precious and semiprecious stones. One of the stones is emerald. This dark green stone is a prized jewel whose value is in the thousands of dollars per carat. If each of the 12 foundation stones were only one foot thick, there would be 2,250,000 square mile layers of each stone a foot thick. How could you ever figure the value of a one-foot thick layer of emerald that covered 2,250,000 square miles?

The 12 entrances into the city are single pearls. The size of the pearls is not given, but they have to be big enough to allow the population of the city to go in and out. The streets passing through the pearls are made of pure gold. The pearls are set in a 300-foot tall wall which is made of jasper, and the wall encircles the entire 6000-mile outer perimeter of the city. The Scriptures also tell us that the light of God shines out through the pure gold siding and causes the city to glow with the glory of God.

**"And the foundations of the wall of the city were garnished with all manner of precious stones. The first foundation was jasper; the second, sapphire; the third, a chalcedony; the fourth, an emerald;**

**The fifth, sardonyx; the sixth, sardius; the seventh, chrysolyte; the eighth, beryl; the ninth, a topaz; the tenth, a chrysoprasus; the eleventh, a jacinth; the twelfth, an amethyst.**

**And the twelve gates were twelve pearls; every several gate was of one pearl: and the street of the city was pure gold, as it were transparent glass."**

**Revelation 21:19-21**

As staggering as the wealth is that God has invested in the structure of the city, it is not what He values. The appraised value of the city is incalculable, but God's treasure is on the inside. On the inside, wide boulevards are paved in gold. There is a river flowing with the water of life that flows from the throne of God. The tree of life grows along the banks of the river and produces a harvest of twelve different kinds of fruit every month. The leaves of the tree are used for the healing of the nations.

There is a treasury there that is filled with more riches than can be imagined. There are mountains, valleys and places in which Christians live with all the saints who have gone before them throughout the ages. The sheer, visual beauty of the city is breathtaking. But even this is still not what God values most.

The focal point of the whole city is the throne room in which the worship services of eternity take place. The majesty of the structure fills the center of the city. Here, the elders of Israel and the apostles of the Church sit on either side of the throne of God, with Jesus sitting at God's right hand. Before them is the altar where Jesus offered His blood when He returned to the Father after His resurrection. Beyond the altar is the sea of glass which is the broad polished floor upon which multitudes gather for worship. Flying above are the four beasts and angels crying, "Holy, Holy, Holy." Around the sea of glass is the largest stadium imaginable, the place in which all the saints are invited to share the presence of God.

Finally, we get to the object of God's affection. Understand that God has prepared this entire city for those who love Him. For us. *We* are the reason God put all of this together. Without the saints the New Jerusalem would be one big, nearly empty city. God values the saints more than all the wealth the city can hold. The Bible says that we are the apple of His eye. After all, the price God paid for our redemption was the greatest possible. If the price says anything about the value of the thing purchased, then we are more valuable to God than we ever imagined.

The eternity we are going to share with Him will not be boring, either. The Scriptures further tell us that we will be going in and out of the city, representing God in various capacities, and that His glory will be on us. The glory that was on Jesus when He appeared to John on the isle of Patmos and on Adam and Eve before their fallen state in the Garden of Eden will be on the saints. If you aren't finding something in all this to motivate you to live a life pleasing to God, please wake up and read this again.

Satan's plan is to destroy your life to the degree that you give up on your eternity. The Holy Spirit was sent from God to help you live your life in such a way as to qualify you for entry into the city. Is there anything this world has to offer that is worth the risk of losing an eternity in the presence of God? Wouldn't it be utter torment to know that such a glorious place exists and you are denied entry?

The Good News is that God loves you so much, He has provided all you need to succeed in this life and in the one to come if you will simply take Him up on His offer. Whatever you do, don't miss out on the greatest offer ever given to mankind. Love God with your whole heart, study His Word, serve your fellow man and keep yourself unpolluted from the world. What is waiting for you is worth more than all the disciplines and heartaches of this life. May God bless your journey with His understanding and give you the strength to meet with the saints in eternity.

> **"According as his divine power hath given unto us all things that pertain unto life and godliness, through the knowledge of him that hath called us to glory and virtue."**
>
> **2 Peter 1:3**

## Discussion Points:

1. Who gets to live in the New Jerusalem?
2. How big is the city?
3. Which one of the physical attributes of the city seems most impressive to you?
4. What does God value the most?

## Memory Verse:

...the Spirit saith unto the churches; To him that overcometh will I give to eat of the tree of life, which is in the midst of the paradise of God.

**Revelation 2:7**

## Lesson #19
# Witnessing

Occasionally in life you find something out of the ordinary that impresses you so much you find yourself wanting to tell everybody about it. When a new restaurant opens near you and the food is exceptional, you feel it is almost your duty to tell your friends so they too can enjoy what you have found. This word-of-mouth advertising is so effective, many businesses depend on it to build their customer base.

This desire to share with others the good news about what you have found is the essence of witnessing. I can't think of any better news to share with people than the fact that they can be forgiven of their sins and can receive the gift of eternal life. Some New Testament Christians got so excited in telling others about their beliefs, they sometimes got into trouble with the religious leaders. Peter and John were called in and threatened with bodily harm if they wouldn't stop telling people Jesus was risen from the dead. Their response was as follows:

> "But Peter and John answered and said unto them, Whether it be right in the sight of God to hearken unto you more than unto God, judge ye.
>
> For we cannot but speak the things which we have seen and heard."
>
> Acts 4:19,20

What they said was simply, "Whether you approve or not, we have to tell what we have seen and heard." Once you have found your peace with God, you too will want to tell what has happened to you. While there are many formalized witnessing plans, the best by far is simply to tell your own story. You don't have to be seminary-trained to stand between sinners and a Godless eternity. All you really need is a genuine concern and the leadership of the Holy Spirit. Remember, one of the main reasons the Holy Spirit was sent into the lives of believers was to empower them to become witnesses.

> **"But ye shall receive power, after that the Holy Ghost is come upon you: and ye shall be witnesses unto me both in Jerusalem, and in all Judaea, and in Samaria, and unto the uttermost part of the earth."**
>
> **Acts 1:8**

It is God's desire that none would perish but that all would have eternal life. The privilege of delivering this glorious message to the world falls on us. For this reason, the Holy Spirit was sent into our lives — to help us be as effective as we can possibly be. One way He helps is by interacting with us through that still small voice in our inner man that gives us direction, information or encouragement as we live our lives. Jesus promised the disciples that when the Holy Spirit was come, He would bring all things to our remembrance concerning Jesus' teachings.

Two truths are glaringly obvious in the promise of the Holy Spirit's ministry. First, we will not reach the world with the Good News with maximum effectiveness unless we have the ministry of the Holy Spirit in our lives. Second, it will be difficult for the Holy Spirit to bring things to our remembrance if we have never learned them in the first place. Part of our preparation

*Witnessing*

in becoming an effective witness is to seek to understand all we can about our own salvation.

**"Study to shew thyself approved unto God, a workman that needeth not to be ashamed, rightly dividing the word of truth."** 2 Timothy 2:15

If you will be diligent to familiarize yourself with the plan of salvation, the Holy Spirit will be faithful to help you clearly and effectively communicate the plan to those who are ready to receive it. The plan is covered in more detail in Lesson #2, but we list it here again as a means of reinforcement. By studying these lessons you are applying and preparing yourself to help someone receive the greatest gift ever offered. Please take the time to read and meditate on the passages of Scripture listed below. They will not only help you more fully understand your own experience, but will also be a resource for the Holy Spirit to use when the time is right to help others.

*Salvation Plan*

1. Acknowledge to God that you are a sinner. (Romans 3:10, 23)

2. Repent. (Decide to stop living your own way and submit your life to God.) (Acts 2:38)

3. Ask God's forgiveness for living outside His laws. (Proverbs 21:2)

4. Accept God's gift of eternal life. (John 10:28)

5. Decide to live the rest of your life in a way that pleases God. (John 14:15)

6. Use the Scriptures to determine how God wants you to live. (2 Timothy 3:16-17)

7. Tell others about your decision. (Matthew 28:19)

*What are the Benefits of Salvation?*

1. Forgiveness — guilt free living (1 John 1:9)

2. Healing  (Isaiah 53:5)

3. Help in living this life here and now  (2 Peter 1:4)

4. Eternal life  (Romans 6:23)

The great commission tells us to go into all the world and preach the gospel. Obviously not everyone can go to every place in the world to tell the Good News. If you are not called to personally go to reach the unsaved in the uttermost parts of the earth, then you should help with prayer and finances in sending those who are called.

You can, however, go into your daily world and share the Gospel there. You meet and work with people every day who may never be exposed to the Gospel of Jesus Christ if they don't hear it from or see it in you. Live your life in such a manner so as to create in others a hunger for the way of life they see in you. In the fullness of time, the Holy Spirit will arrange divine appointments to let you know without a doubt it is time to witness to those around you.

You will find that, when one of these divine appointments occurs, all your studying, prayer and preparation will merge in partnership with the Holy Spirit. He will reach through you to offer the gift of salvation to the needy soul. This experience of working with God to offer eternal life will be one of the most rewarding of your life as a Christian.

Your life may be the only Bible some people ever read, your words the only sermon they ever hear, the way you live your life the only witness they ever know. This realization will cause you to rejoice in the opportunity to be used by God, to live the life of a witness before your world every day. When you stand before Him and hear Him say, *"Well done,"* you will have all the reward you need.

## Discussion Points:

1. What does the word *witness* mean?
2. What is the role of the Holy Spirit in witnessing?
3. How can you go into all the world and preach the Gospel?
4. What should we do to reach those in the uttermost parts of the earth?

## Memory Verse:

**But ye shall receive power, after that the Holy Ghost is come upon you: and ye shall be witnesses unto Me both in Jerusalem, and in all Judaea, and in Samaria, and unto the uttermost part of the earth.**

**Acts 1:8**

## Lesson #20
# Communion

For most of us the word communion brings to mind the Lord's Supper. The pictures of Jesus and His disciples, sitting around a table sharing a last meal before His crucifixion, are common sights in churches around the world. Yet as tender and touching as that last meal was, it was symbolic of something much more significant than friends saying goodbye. As you study the Scriptures, you will find that often God uses physical events to deliver a much stronger spiritual message. Such is the case with the Last Supper which Jesus shared with His followers.

Remember that when Jesus took time to participate in an event, there was a reason. Jesus' life was a lesson for us from His birth to His death. When He and the disciples shared that last meal, Jesus was living out the fulfillment of prophecy. In order to understand how this event was intended to speak to us today, let's briefly look at just what this meal was.

"Then came the day of unleavened bread, when the passover must be killed.

And he sent Peter and John, saying, Go and prepare us the passover, that we may eat.

And they said unto him, Where wilt thou that we prepare?

And he said unto them, Behold, when ye are entered into the city, there shall a man meet you, bearing a pitcher of water; follow him into the house where he entereth in.

And ye shall say unto the goodman of the house, The Master saith unto thee, Where is the guest chamber, where I shall eat the passover with my disciples?

And he shall shew you a large upper room furnished: there make ready.

And they went, and found as he had said unto them: and they made ready the passover.

And when the hour was come, he sat down, and the twelve apostles with him.

And he said unto them, With desire I have desired to eat this passover with you before I suffer:

For I say unto you, I will not any more eat thereof, until it be fulfilled in the kingdom of God.

And he took the cup, and gave thanks, and said, Take this, and divide it among yourselves:

For I say unto you, I will not drink of the fruit of the vine, until the kingdom of God shall come.

And he took bread, and gave thanks, and brake it, and gave unto them, saying, This is my body which is given for you: this do in remembrance of me.

Likewise also the cup after supper, saying, This cup is the new testament in my blood, which is shed for you."

**Luke 22:7-20**

During the meal, Jesus took some of the unleavened bread and broke it to distribute it to His disciples. After that He took a cup of wine (or grape juice) and gave it to them to drink. These events at another meal wouldn't have been that unusual. But this was not just another meal.

This meal that they shared was the celebration of the feast of Passover. The feast originally began when the children of Israel were in captivity in Egypt and God was about to deliver them from their 430 years of captivity. The night before they left Egypt, God instructed Moses to have every family sacrifice a lamb. The blood of the lamb was to be spread on the doorposts of the house, and they were to cook and eat the lamb as a last meal before their deliverance. Later that night, when the death angel passed through Egypt, he was instructed to pass over or bypass every house that had obeyed the instructions to sacrifice the lamb and place the blood on the doorposts. In the households which had not obeyed, the first born of the house died.

That was a night like none other. While the Israelites obeyed God and feasted together, God's judgment was on the nation of Egypt. Tens of thousands of the first born of Egypt died that night. The next day, the grief was so overwhelming in Egypt that Pharaoh let the Israelites leave to go to the Promised Land. That Passover feast had been the last supper before the Israelite's deliverance.

When Jesus and His disciples prepared their last supper together, it was no coincidence that it was on the Passover feast. Read what the Bible says before Jesus distributed the bread to his disciples:

> **"And when he had given thanks, he brake it, and said, Take, eat: this is my body, which is broken for you...."**
>
> **1 Corinthians 11:24**

He knew full well that His body was about to be broken in His sacrifice for the sins of the world. In the same way He took the cup and said,

**"This cup is the new testament in my blood, which is shed for you."**
                                                              **Luke 22:20**

Make no mistake, Jesus was completely aware of the fact that He was there to become the sacrificial lamb. He was to offer His own blood and broken body to fulfill the requirements in the payment for the sins of the world. He became the Passover lamb so that when the judgment of God fell on a sinful world, that judgment would pass over all who had received Him, just like the angel of death passed over the houses of the obedient in Egypt.

Jesus knew in advance that He was the payment, and yet, He chose to share that last meal with His disciples, committing Himself to be that sacrifice. The disciples had no idea that this was indeed their last supper together before their deliverance from the captivity of sin. When Jesus died on the cross and shed His blood, the Scriptures say that the handwriting of ordinances against us was blotted out and nailed to His cross (Colossians 2:14).

By becoming our Passover lamb, Jesus spiritually applies His own blood to the doorposts of our lives. When Satan or others try to judge us, that judgment must pass over us. We have been wonderfully delivered from the cruel taskmaster of sin.

If the disciples had been aware of what was about to happen, they might have responded differently when they went to the garden to pray with Jesus after dinner. The significance of those moments just before Jesus' arrest brought the presence of ministering angels. They encouraged Jesus to be faithful to the end. While this was going on, the disciples slept.

Let me help you be fully awake to the meaning of this event in your life. When Jesus died for your sins, God accepted His sacrifice to redeem you from the captivity of sin. The curse that came to all mankind through Adam's disobedience brought fear, sickness, rebellion, sexual impurity, separation from God and all manner of problems to the human race.

I would like for you to read the full account of the communion message. It's a wonderful passage of Scripture.

> "For I have received of the Lord that which also I delivered unto you, That the Lord Jesus the same night in which he was betrayed took bread:
>
> And when he had given thanks, he brake it, and said, Take, eat: this is my body, which is broken for you: this do in remembrance of me.
>
> After the same manner also he took the cup, when he had supped, saying, This cup is the new testament in my blood: this do ye, as oft as ye drink it, in remembrance of me.
>
> For as often as ye eat this bread, and drink this cup, ye do shew the Lord's death till he come.
>
> Wherefore whosoever shall eat this bread, and drink this cup of the Lord, unworthily, shall be guilty of the body and blood of the Lord.
>
> But let a man examine himself, and so let him eat of that bread, and drink of that cup.
>
> For he that eateth and drinketh unworthily, eateth and drinketh damnation to himself, not discerning the Lord's body.

> For this cause many are weak and sickly among you, and many sleep.
>
> For if we would judge ourselves, we should not be judged."
>
> 1 Corinthians 11:23-31

Why are people weak, sick and dead from not properly discerning the Lord's body? God reached down to man through Jesus and offered the provision for lifting the curse. Although the provision is paid for, if it is not accepted, it is of no benefit. You must understand that salvation includes more than the forgiveness of your sins. It also includes the cancellation of the consequences of sin. If the wages of sin is death, then the acceptance of the forgiveness of sin brings life. That life isn't just eternal life. It also includes blessing in this life. To understand what Jesus bought for us is to properly discern the payment made on Calvary by the sacrifice of the Lord's body.

When faith is mixed with understanding about this event, you can then accept all that God intended to give you. Peace, joy, forgiveness, healing, finances and everything else which is offered by God can be accepted. This wonderful provision of Calvary is celebrated in communion.

By first looking inside yourself to make sure there is nothing offensive to the Lord, you can then eat the bread and drink of the cup of remembrance of the Lord's death with a clear conscience. Taking communion with a clean heart allows you to express your gratitude for all that you have been given and for all that you have been forgiven. The opportunity to judge yourself allows you to avoid being judged with the world. Such self-examination and grateful worship during the communion experience allow you to stand clean and humble before God each time you participate. What a blessing!

*Discussion Points:*

1. How did the Passover begin?
2. How did Jesus become our Passover Lamb?
3. What do the bread and wine of communion represent?
4. How do we properly discern the Lord's body?

*Memory Verse:*

**But let a man examine himself, and so let him eat of that bread, and drink of that cup.**
**1 Corinthians 11:28**

For more information about this ministry, please contact:

**Books for Children of the World**
6701 N. Bryant
Oklahoma City, OK 73121
voice – 405/721-7417
fax – 405/478-4352
website – www.adoptalamb.org